Longmans' English Classics

# EMERSON'S ESSAYS

ON

# MANNERS, SELF-RELIANCE, COMPENSATION, NATURE, FRIENDSHIP

EDITED

WITH NOTES AND AN INTRODUCTION

BY

EUNICE J. CLEVELAND, A. M.

HEAD OF THE ENGLISH DEPARTMENT, NORTHROP COLLEGIATE SCHOOL,
MINNEAPOLIS, MINN.

LONGMANS, GREEN, AND CO.

FOURTH AVENUE AND 30TH STREET, NEW YORK

PRAIRIE AVENUE & 25TH STREET, CHICAGO

1915

# CONTENTS

# INTRODUCTION

## I. LIFE OF EMERSON

(May 25, 1803—April 27, 1882)

We have few more intimate biographical records than Emerson's; fewer still that cause so little disappointment in the reading. In the wealth of material at hand,—in his Journal and letters as well as in the personal reminiscences of a great band of friends and admirers,—we are brought face to face with a personality that can but win by the "cumulative power of character." Even those who met Emerson with prejudices to be overcome were conquered by his presence. "In an instant all my dislike vanished," said Crabbe Robinson, in reporting the first glimpse caught of him across a crowded room. One and another bear evidence to the same personal power with a concurrence that would be tiresome, were it not for the strong individual conviction in each case.

Two other brothers, Edward and Charles, both younger, shared this power; William, the oldest, was likewise gifted with unusual intellect. The family lived in Boston, where the father, William Emerson, was a brilliant Congregational minister, prominent in religious, social, and literary circles till his death in 1811. That event put a new face on the circumstances of the family; only the most rigid and careful economy, supplemented by the generous continuance of part of her husband's salary and the help of relatives, enabled the mother, Ruth Haskins Emerson, to keep the family together and give them the education due to their great intellectual gifts and to the traditions of the family. "They were born to be educated," their aunt, Mary Moody Emerson, once declared.

This aunt was a force to be reckoned with. Odd to the point of absurdity, she yet had so fine an intellect and so true a nature that she gained and held the respect of her nephews. She was at times an inmate of their home; at other times her peculiarities drove her to the quiet of the country. But absent or present, she continually urged them on by the spur of her spiritual ambition to live lives of independent thought, to disregard fame and social advancement, and to fit themselves for true leadership. The early correspondence between her and Ralph Waldo Emerson is scarcely less valuable than the first few years of his Journal in tracing the rise of his fine independence of thought.

Through a childhood filled with work and books, seasoned by the hardships of poverty, and straitened by Puritan discipline, one catches glimpses of the Emerson of later days. He made efforts at poetical and oratorical composition, flat and feeble to be sure, but earnest; and when, in his twelfth year, the family went to live for a time with their step-grandfather, Dr. Ezra Ripley, at the Old Manse in Concord, Waldo and his two younger brothers were set free in nature. "They took that valley for their toy," writes Emerson in *The Dirge,* and alludes to games that filled the Concord woods and cornfields with echoes from the past. When he came back as a man, those woods were already dear to him; and the imagination that in boyhood had wakened through them to a love of nature, found there in manhood as nowhere else, a way of feeling and seeing that deepened into philosophical vision.

In the Latin School at Boston Emerson did not distinguish himself; but at fourteen he was ready for Harvard. William had preceded him there, and later the two younger boys followed him. All were obliged to mingle study and work and to live more frugally than was good for boys of their delicate constitution. On entrance Emerson was President's Freshman, or messenger, and later eked out his expenses by waiting on table, tutoring, and teaching a country school. He was urged on meanwhile by the stern-spirited women at home to rise above material inconveniences and become an independent, moral spirit. Those who knew him described him even in his freshman days as "kindly, affable, and self contained." He took his degree in 1821 without any distinction except the rather equivocal one of being chosen class poet after seven others had refused the office; but though he bore from college little honor and less knowledge of mathematics, he had "consoled himself for his defects," as his Journal long years afterwards states, "with Chaucer and Montaigne, with Plutarch and Plato at night." Other authors we find mentioned here and there as forming part of this privately acquired education,—Otway, Massinger, Swift, Addison, Sterne, and many historical writers and poets of his own day. Shakespeare he knew from beginning to end.

After graduation he turned to teaching in earnest, assisting in a school for young ladies which William, "a grave professor even at eighteen," had started in his mother's house. In a short time he was left in sole charge by William's departure for Europe. The task was far from congenial, for he fell short of his brother's dignity and was often teased for his bashfulness and blushing cheeks by his roguish pupils. In after years they praised his work as a teacher, but he looked upon it with regret because he had made it too much a matter of dry form, keeping the best of his thoughts to himself. His Journal of those days shows that even then he was cherishing ideas which were to become an important part of his later philosophy.

He continued his teaching till free from debt, then in 1825 went back to Harvard to study theology. But he made the mistake, for the sake of economy, of taking a damp, dimly lighted room. Rheumatism, weak eyes, and a stricture in the chest were the results, so that in 1826 when he was "approbated" as a Unitarian minister, he was in a fair way to be a confirmed invalid. Rev. Samuel Ripley, the uncle who had always stood behind the family most generously, sent him south. Lazy days in St. Augustine restored his general health, though his lungs were long weak. But prudence and "hope," as his son has said, conquered ill-health at last, and set him free for his life work.

After the preliminaries usual to a young man starting out in the ministry, Emerson at the age of twenty-six was ordained assistant to Rev. Mr. Ware of the Second Church, Boston, and soon succeeded to the sole pastorship. The same year, 1829, he married Ellen Tucker of Concord, New Hampshire, a joyous, gracious woman, whose influence it is easy to trace in several passages in the essays of this book. One of Emerson's parishioners describes her as a flowerlike woman whose delicate health made her practically a recluse from the start; once each Sunday they saw her when she came in a carriage to hear her husband's sermon. These years of Emerson's pastorate have an ever-increasing interest to the student of his life. They were outwardly prosperous, free from the hardships of early years and from anxiety for his family. But the outer events sink into insignificance before the importance of the mental life he was living. The long lists of books suggested by the Journal of those years show that he was pursuing a course of study that was bringing him into the great current of the thought of his age. The number and variety of these literary influences must have proved distracting to a less balanced intellect, but to Emerson they were all leading quietly to one belief that was to give direction to his whole life. He was making a thoughtful comparative study of the old Greek philosophers and the modern thinkers in the same line, with close attention to psychology and science. His favorite authors still appear in the lists, but several are added,—Landor, Goethe, Carlyle, and Swedenborg. The sense of the beauty and harmony of the world that had often wakened him at night when he was a boy with a feeling of indescribable happiness, was deepened by this reading; and to it was added a growing reverence for the mysterious working of man's mind. The sermons in which he gave public expression to these thoughts are unpublished, but those who have read them in manuscript describe them as conventional in tone, differing little from the usual sermon of his day and church. Those who heard them, however, say they had a singular power of making the life of everyday seem new and very real.

The years of this service were limited. In 1831 Mrs. Emerson died. September of the following year ended Emerson's connection with his church. He proposed that they should adopt a simpler form of the communion service in which the elements of bread and wine should not be used. He had come to feel acutely that for him worship must be absolutely free from formalism, and if the church did not adopt his suggestion he must resign. But the church stood by the traditional form, although there was no unkindliness of spirit on either side. In December Emerson, practically severed from the profession for which he had been preparing all his life, set sail for Europe. His farewell letter to his church is the best comment on the situation; one feels on reading it that he would always be a leader of men's thoughts whether he held a pulpit or not.

Of his European trip we have an account in his Journal and letters, and in the beginning of *English Traits*. He went by way of the Mediterranean and traveled northward through Italy. The churches made a great impression upon him; again and again he describes the feeling of awe they awakened. His comments on Italian art are full of self-revelation: "I make a continual effort not to be pleased except by that which ought to please *me*," he notes in Florence, "and I walked coolly round and round the marble lady"; "I collect nothing that can be touched or tasted or smelled, neither cameo, painting, nor medallion, but I value much the growing picture which the ages have painted and which I reverently survey." Throughout his journey his supreme interest was in men. He reconstructed in his imagination the cities of the past and brought their heroes back to walk their streets; and he visited the great men of the present. In Florence he became acquainted with Landor, and in England he saw Coleridge and Wordsworth.

But the event of his journey was his visit to Carlyle, then comparatively unknown. He made his way from Dumfries to Craigenputtock, where he found the "tall, gaunt man of clifflike brow" with whom he had formed a book acquaintance in America. He stayed only over night, but he "talked and heard talk to his heart's content," as Carlyle wrote to his mother. One may well believe it from the range of topics that were discussed in the short visit, from favorite books to "that plastic little animal man" and the immortality of the soul. In August he wrote to Mr. Ireland after his visit to Carlyle, "The comfort of meeting a man is that he speaks sincerely, . . . that he is above the meanness of pretending to knowledge which he has not." He had not found Carlyle all that he had expected, but he had found him a man, and the two sealed a lifelong friendship. It was Emerson who first published *Sartor Resartus* in its non-periodical form, and later other works of Carlyle, sparing neither time nor expense in the service of his friend. Carlyle for his part interested himself in Emerson's literary success in England. The friendship is left to us in permanent record in one of the most interesting books of the nineteenth century, *The Correspondence of Carlyle and Emerson.*

In 1833 Emerson returned to America, confirmed in his determination to wait patiently the issue of events. Already he was revolving plans for his first book. He settled in Concord, drawn partly by his brother Charles's influence and partly by his boyhood love of the place. It was convenient also to East Lexington, where he accepted a call to act as temporary pastor. He and his mother first lived in the Old Manse; but in 1835, upon his engagement to Lydian Jackson, he bought the house on the old stage road to Boston which became his home for the rest of his life. The early days in Concord were saddened by news of the death of his brother Edward, for whom Emerson had cherished an almost adoring admiration. The youngest brother Charles did not long survive; he died two years later, in 1836. Him Emerson describes as "clean and sweet in life, untempted almost." The loss of these brothers was too sore ever to be repaired, for they had been from earliest years so closely bound to Emerson that it was as if a part of his mental faculty had gone with them. He bore their death bravely, as he had borne that of his wife, but it is undeniable that to this bereavement must be traced in some measure that gentle reticence of spirit which marked his social intercourse outside his own family circle.

Emerson began his literary career in 1836 with the publication of *Nature*, "the azure book" that Carlyle welcomed with warm praise as a foundation for work of real value to the race. Carlyle's prophecy proved true, but at first there were few who shared his enthusiasm. This first book of Emerson may almost be called an epitome of his later teaching. It is remarkable as well for the beauty of its expression; many of its passages are prose poetry of delicate but inspiring imagination.

Two years earlier, by speaking before the Mechanic Institute of Boston, Emerson had entered on the field of lecturing. New England lyceums, called into existence by a general desire for culture, attracted many speakers from home and abroad, but none who exerted a deeper influence than he. Almost every year as long as his health permitted him, he delivered lecture courses in Boston. At first he gave besides only an occasional address in his own village or in some other New England town, but gradually his engagements called him farther and farther from home,—to New York, Philadelphia, Pittsburgh, and westward, until after 1850 he made trips even beyond the Mississippi. In the winter of 1847-48 he gave a series of courses in England and Scotland. Of Emerson as a lecturer we have many descriptions. He was singularly impressive, though his manner was quiet and his style unoratorical. He read from notes, handling his manuscripts with hesitation and looking out over his audience with a farseeing gaze that was at once kindly and remote. He had his hearers with him from the start, even those who did not understand what he was saying, and passed from one of his quaintly humorous illustrations to his gravest teachings without a break in their responsive attention. The compelling principle was his high, serene character; that was "the something deeper than his words" to which Lowell alludes in his essay on Emerson as a lecturer. It spoke in every word and in his quiet presence, but especially in his voice,—"that undertow of the rich baritone that swept minds from their foothold into deeper waters with a drift they could not and would not resist." By force of this quiet, impressive personality Emerson made the lecture platform take the place of the pulpit he had left, and in a few years ceased even to serve as supply, devoting himself instead to this lay preaching. His lecture work extended over a period of forty-seven years, the last address being that of 1881.

Two of his addresses deserve especial mention as of historical importance. One is *The American Scholar*, the Phi Beta Kappa oration of 1837; and the other the address before the senior class of Divinity College, Cambridge, in 1838. The first because of its strong appeal for a truly American thought and literature has been called "our intellectual Declaration of Independence." The second is scarcely less significant in its bearing on religious history. In it Emerson eloquently urges the need for simplifying and spiritualizing faith. This address set a ban upon his religious teaching and closed the doors of Harvard against him for nearly thirty years. The change of sentiment wrought during that time is marked by the fact that at the close he was given the honorary degree of LL.D., was made an Overseer of the college, and was invited again to deliver the Phi Beta Kappa address.

The record of the thirty years that worked the change is quiet, but not uneventful, though the events are of a nature that gain little from a brief telling. They concern themselves, aside from his literary work, chiefly with the placid family and neighborhood life of Concord. Emerson was at his best in his home. He was very fond of children, and to the three who remained to him after the death of his eldest child, Waldo, he gave a most delightful companionship. Few passages in his letters are finer than those in which he sends messages from England to the children at home. As a townsman he fulfilled his duties faithfully. The bucket of the fire department, his son says, was always in the entry, and he was long a member of the school committee. He was particularly interested in the town-meeting, holding it in respect as a typical American institution; but he seldom spoke there, and indeed carried himself always as a modest, retiring householder. Nevertheless the rank and file of the townsmen, those who gathered on the corner or before the tavern to discuss important topics, stood in awe of him. At the appearance of his tall, slender figure the group melted away or stood tongue-tied. Emerson never blamed them, though he had a philosopher's interest in the wisdom he might have gathered from their talk. From the more substantial neighbors, upright New Englanders of the old type, he won not only respect but pleasant companionship.

Concord of those days, however, could offer friendships of a more unusual type; it was rich in personalities of extreme interest. One of these was Henry Thoreau.

For two years he lived most democratically as a general helper in Emerson's household; at another time he made his home in a cabin in Walden woods. So devoted was he to his revered friend that it is said he came to speak in the same remarkable voice. There is little in the Journal that betokens more genuine pleasure than the pages which record the woodland expeditions Emerson took with this eccentric naturalist. "The rivergod has taken the form of my valiant Henry Thoreau here, and introduced me to the riches of his shadowy, starlit, moonlit stream, a lovely new world lying as close and yet as unknown to this vulgar trite one, as death to life, or poetry to prose. Through one field we went to the boat, and then left all time, all science, all history behind us and entered into nature with one stroke of a paddle." Another interesting neighbor was Bronson Alcott, the visionary philosopher and author of the *Orphic Sayings.* With him Emerson enjoyed a finer intellectual companionship than with anyone except Carlyle. Alcott and Thoreau, he said, were the only ones besides himself, who really knew the law of Compensation; but Alcott's mind lacked conversation so that no one would ever know its riches as he did. Another ardent thinker whom Emerson counted among his friends was Margaret Fuller, the high-souled, adventurous woman whose life ended so tragically in 1850. With her intercourse was more stormy. She could never accept quietly the reticence of Emerson's nature, and accused him of "always seeming to be on stilts." "It is even so," he comments, "but having never found any remedy, I am very patient with this folly." Hawthorne became a neighbor in 1842 when he came to live at the Old Manse. He was so shy that though he often walked home with Emerson, he could but rarely be persuaded to come into the house. The two never came into close relations, though Emerson always honored Hawthorne's noble character, and looked forward to the time when they should be friends. "I thought I could well wait his time and mine for what was so well worth waiting," he wrote to Mrs. Hawthorne when death had put an end to the hope.

The wholesome Concord life with its stimulating companionships and simple social relations was a fitting accompaniment to Emerson's real work. Every day he spent hours in his study, "reading for lustres," he said; every day also he walked alone, usually in his little wood on Walden Pond, giving himself up to meditation and the quiet influence of nature. The fruits of his thought, first given to the world in lectures, began to appear in print in 1841, when Emerson issued his second book, *Essay, First Series,* followed in 1844 by the *Second Series.* The two Series included, among others, the five essays in this volume. In the mean time Emerson had been making frequent contributions to the *Dial,* the magazine of high ideals and short life, which was started in 1840 under the editorship of Margaret Fuller. In 1843 he himself reluctantly assumed the editorship and carried the paper its last two years. In 1847 he published *May Day and Other Poems;* in 1849 *Nature, Addresses and Lectures,* and in 1850 *Representative Men.* Without doubt this decade was his most important period of literary activity. Interesting and valuable as the four later volumes of essays are, the measure of his genius and the strength of his teaching may be found in the books mentioned. They were received with enthusiasm. Editions were at once issued in England, and reissues were in demand there, and in America as well. They passed over to the continent also and were translated by enthusiastic admirers. All hailed Emerson as the great thinker who proved that America could produce a genius all her own.

About the time that Emerson brought out his first volume of essays, he became interested in two social experiments. One of these was the famous Brook Farm, ten or twelve miles from Boston. The men who organized this scheme were influenced by the same philosophical ideas as Emerson; but they had read also certain continental writers on Socialism, particularly Fourier, who counseled the division of society into phalanxes that should work together for a common living. From 1841 to 1847 work and life and education went on at Brook Farm in a pleasant idyllic course, which was not, however, wholly free from financial embarrassment. Some phases of the life are familiar through Hawthorne's *Blithedale Romance,* but for others one must turn to the personal reminiscences of its members and its visitors. The experiment finally died a natural death, and all that was left was the memory of a pleasant bit of poetry that had lived itself out on New England soil. In the mean time the other community had sped an even shorter course. This was Fruitlands, where Alcott had gathered a little company of men, some from beyond the sea. As was to be expected from a man of his character, his system of farming was comically impractical, so that his experiment was a failure from the start.

Emerson was a frequent visitor at both communities. He had in fact thought seriously of accepting the earnest invitation to live at Brook Farm. The character of the experimenters and their unselfish aims could not fail to excite his respect, but his dislike of anything like organized reform and his shrewd common sense kept him quietly at home. He tried, it is true, a few socialistic experiments on his own account. In one he was soon convinced that the maids could eat apart from his family without imperiling democratic principles, especially when they sensibly preferred to. In another he found that he could not work his own garden, and afterward read or write with any degree of success. So he settled back into his usual mode of life, satisfied with comfortable conventionality; but he could view with sympathetic amusement the more extensive experiments going on at the two farms. His visits found vent in humorous entries in his Journal. "The fault of Alcott's community," he wrote, "is that it has only room for one;" and of Brook Farm he recorded, "One man ploughed all day, and one looked out of the window all day and drew his picture, and both received the same wages."

If Emerson had a large measure of respect for these experimenters, he had much less in common with the crowds of erratic reformers who brought their wild schemes to the famous man of Concord in hopes of his becoming a convert. He received the fanatics with a fine and patient courtesy, though their importunity made distracting breaks in his time; but they had no other satisfaction from their visits.

There was one class of strangers, however, to whom he always extended a free and cordial welcome. In a letter to Miss Peabody he wrote, "My special parish is young men inquiring their way in life." Even in his last working days, when prudence counseled conservation of his powers, to all the young pilgrims drawn from far and near to Concord he gave a welcome and a chance to prove whether they were in truth men. One of them characterizes Emerson's attitude toward young men as "wonderfully flattering; it was a manner I know no name for but expectancy; as if the world problem was now to be solved and we were the beardless Œdipuses for whom he had been faithfully waiting." Another says, "Almost before we were alone he had made me forget in whose presence I stood. . . . He addressed me as if I were wholly impersonal, a sort of invisible audience, . . . He always talked slowly, and his words had the trick of impressing themselves which belongs to happy selection; but it was mostly because his speech was so wise and sincere and came from the depths of his heart, that it has sunken so deep into mine." He was ever lured on, as he wrote Carlyle, "with the hope of saying something which shall stick by the good boys." But to two principles he firmly adhered in this intercourse. He always spoke in the tone and style that was his own with no false allowance for youth; those for whom it was meant could understand it, he held. And he never encouraged disciples; it was his supreme duty to tell people what line of thought he was following in his search for wisdom, and to report as faithfully as he could the truths revealed to him, but every youth must search for himself and be not an Emersonian but an individual.

Only once in his life did Emerson come forward and offer himself as a direct leader of men's thought. That was in the great abolition struggle. From this at first he held himself aloof, partly out of dislike for the methods that were used and partly because he could always see both sides of a question. He long counseled settlement of the difficulty by the purchase of the slaves at whatsoever cost or sacrifice. This he would follow by the slow process of education and general enlightenment. But in 1850 his Journal begins to show that a different phase of the question was rousing him; "These taunts upon sentimentalism, and higher law, and the like, which our Senators use, are the screens of their cowardice." It was as a champion, then, against the moral cowardice of truckling to the demands of property that he finally came forward into the struggle. From then on to the close of the war he had for every crisis a fitting word, fair and liberal, but unbending for the right as he saw it. When the Harvard boys came back from war, he spoke the Commemoration address for those who were left behind. It was fitting that he should, for as Lowell said, "To him more than to all other causes did they owe the sustaining strength of their thoughtful heroism." It was his last patriotic address in connection with the great struggle.

In 1867 Emerson published in the *Atlantic Monthly* his *Terminus,* in which he expressed his conviction:

> "It is time to be old.
> The port, well worth the cruise, is near."

Others had not recognized that fact concerning him, but he knew. He completed tasks after that, but most of them were more in the nature of gathering together what he had already done than of fresh composition. In 1870-71 he gave two courses of lectures in philosophy at Harvard, in which he hoped to carry out a plan that had entered his head in 1837,—to put in permanent, consistent form his teaching that the laws of the soul parallel the laws of external nature. But the task was beyond his waning powers. In 1872 the burning of his home and a low fever that assailed him from the incident exposure, still further worked upon his strength. Friends sent him abroad, while they restored the house in minute detail. But his real work was over. What addresses he gave after that were possible only through the assistance of his friend Mr. Cabot and his daughter Ellen, who supplied the lapses in his failing memory. This failure took the form of an inability to recall words, usually of common meaning, an inability he was wont to cover by quaint, roundabout expressions. "Isn't there too much heaven on you there?" he asked a friend whom he thought uncomfortable in the blazing sun. He still read, still talked with those in whose presence he was free, and to the last cherished the thought of friends whose names he could no longer remember. "That is *that* man, my man," he said of a picture of Carlyle on his study wall. His old age even to its last tranquil breath belongs to the well-nigh perfect integrity of his life.

## II. EMERSON'S TEACHING.

In his essays Emerson is a teacher. He offers great moral lessons about what life is and how men should live it, but he does this by suggestion rather than by direct advice, and he does not offer a system of thought. Instead he makes statements of separate truths. Often these stand in very disconnected relations, sometimes one statement is quite inconsistent with another; but a close study of a considerable body of his work, even of the essays of this book, is sufficient to show that these scattered precepts have really a basis of logic and may all be unified by a thorough understanding of a few leading ideas.

In the first place Emerson was an idealist. This means he held that the spirit is real. Some people find it difficult to understand this point of view, for they believe that only what the eye can see and the hand can touch is real. Emerson's idealism is kept in touch with this everyday feeling by a peculiar strain of practicality.

"Nature is ideal to me so long as I cannot try the accuracy of my own senses." "The advantage of the ideal theory is that it presents the world in precisely the view most desirable to the mind." "It animates me to create my own world through the purification of my soul." That last sentence, if looked at closely, offers an insight into his belief. If within a man's own mind is a spirit that can work upon him until the whole world is transformed for him, then that spirit must be real, and the world subordinated to it.

On this theory that the spirit is real has been built up a system of thought that is very old. It is not easy to understand, for like all philosophical systems it deals with very abstract and very lofty ideas. But one must gain some knowledge of it to comprehend the full force of Emerson's teaching, which springs from this system of thought. The two basic principles of the system, as Emerson himself explains them in several places, are Identity and Variety. I. Identity, or Unity, means that the whole universe is one because it is an expression of one Spirit. This Spirit Emerson usually calls Reason, or Intuition. II. Variety, or Motion, signifies the changing forms through which this supreme Reason manifests itself. (*a.*) The flow of Reason through the minds of men is one phase of this manifestation. (*b.*) The great laws and principles that underlie all nature is another. Visible nature, that is everything outside of man's mind, thus becomes a mere symbol, or outer expression, of those laws; or in other words, it is a symbol of universal Reason.

On this underlying unity of man and nature idealists built up the idea that the great physical laws which rule in the outer world are paralleled by moral laws which rule in the minds and lives of men. They believed, for instance, that the law of Fluidity, or constant motion in nature, was a symbol of the constant energy of Reason in man's mind; that the law of Evolution was a symbol of an upward tendency in the moral world; and that the law of Polarity, which balances or neutralizes opposite forces in nature, taught that every act or thought of man would bring to pass its own due reward or penalty.

In the second place Emerson is an individualist. His individualism is an outgrowth of his idealism, for he holds that every person, being different from every other, is fitted to receive and respond to the flow of Reason in his mind, so as to do a work in the world that no other human being can. The individualist has therefore a supreme duty to be free from all overpowering influences from without and listen only to his own Reason. Great men of the past were those who had most clearly fulfilled this duty. It was very important that it should be fulfilled because Reason could act only upon the individual and never upon the masses except through him. He, then, was responsible for improvement in society. In this whole doctrine Emerson is truly American, for his individualism received emphasis from his nationality, and formed the strong point in all the teaching he directed to his countrymen.

In the third place Emerson is an optimist. This is the great prevailing note of his philosophy, as it was the great winning element in his character. He saw in nature the law of compensation working the perfect justice of the Spirit, and this he read as a symbol of the same perfect justice in the lives of men. Reason always triumphs, he said. He saw also in nature the law of evolution working itself out, lower forms ever giving place to higher and tending upward to man. In this he saw a symbol of the evolution possible in the mind of each individual. Sometime would come the age of the perfect man, he said. This doctrine was very American, closely related to the comparatively pure atmosphere of life in the New World and to America's chance for a great future; through it Emerson impressed his own high, far-reaching aims upon his nation.

As was intimated at the start, the system of thought, here given in its barest outline, has its roots far back in the past. Its fundamental ideas of Identity and Variety are traceable to the old Greek schools of philosophy, but the systematizing of it was due largely to Plato. He gave too an abiding literary expression to the idealists' great teaching that the only real life is the life of the spirit, and must concern itself with thought and character. The neo-Platonists and Christian mystics emphasized the mystical union of Reason in man with the universal Reason; and modern philosophers in the light of modern science have worked out many interesting phases of the idealistic theories. To be more explicit as to the exact sources of special idealistic theories is not necessary here. The point to be kept in mind is that this accumulated body of thought was brought into great prominence a little before Emerson was born and in his early years by a number of philosophers and poets. Among them, because of their great influence on the course of literature, may be mentioned Coleridge and Goethe.

This noble heritage was not Emerson's alone. The early nineteenth century writers who had voiced the idealistic tendency had mostly finished their work before he began his, but they had handed the thought on to new workers. It had undergone changes in this transition. The great passion for a sudden perfecting of the human race which had animated many at the time of the French Revolution had faded naturally in the march of historical events, and a quieter view of life had taken its place. One must take things as they were and make the best of them. But if society could not be instantaneously changed, much was to be gained by rousing the individual to live the life of the spirit. Carlyle, who began his literary work in 1824, was of this later school. He spoke the necessity of a healthy, sturdy, sane individual, a man of elemental force, who could pierce with his shrewd eye the shams of life and live in reality. If life looked dark, let him not question too much what it all meant, but find some useful work and do it. Ruskin, beginning in 1843, defended the same fundamental principles though in a different way, for he had the more active instinct of a reformer to fight against existing circumstances. He weighed, however, the finer things of life,—art, science, pity, and usefulness to others,—against all the material advantages in the world. Among the idealistic poets Browning was one of the foremost advocates of the life of the spirit. His subtly drawn portraits picture the souls of men and women. Some are pure and radiant like little Pippa's, shedding a redeeming light on all around; others are scenes of struggles between good and evil; but the lesson is always the prevailing power of Love. The great novelists of the time also were filled with the same spirit. Their noblest characters are those who forget themselves and live simply or grandly for others. Social ties and advantages sink before the power of the soul, and the "happy ending" of the old stories gives way to the triumph of character.

The system of thought of which we have been speaking had a development in America that was modified, naturally, by the conditions existing there. Two of its manifestations deserve especial mention from the relations they bear to Emerson's teaching. One was Transcendentalism. This was not a sudden outburst, for idealistic ideas had long been working in New England thought; but at the time when Emerson's lectures began to attract wide attention these ideas suddenly took a public form. The movement is always associated with Emerson's name, for the teachings of which it was an expression were in the main identical with his. The Transcendentalists were eager, high-souled natures, often so carried away by their ardor as to be fanatical against what they considered the senseless conventions and base aims of society. Many of them were not primarily philosophers; rather they were social reformers, for they had imbibed socialistic ideas along with their idealism and were bent therefore on driving materialism out of society by organized attacks. They divided into sects as numerous as they were enthusiastic, each with its own favorite scheme for improving conditions, and for years they made New England the scene of ardent reform. Mention has already been made of the slight community of interest between Emerson and this active type of Transcendentalists. From the very nature of his teaching he was held aloof from them; his individualism made organized reform of any kind distasteful, and his optimistic belief in the slow triumph of right in society bade him look toward a less direct method of attack.

The second manifestation showed how strange a form idealism might take when developed on American soil. Walt Whitman's first issue of *Leaves of Grass* appeared in 1855. and from then on until his death in 1892 he was a leading figure in American literature. His teachings were fundamentally Emerson's,—idealism, individualism, and optimism,—but he carried them to the extreme of robustness, unconventionality, and democracy. There was no lack of emphasis upon the reality of the life of the spirit, but side by side with that was a sturdy insistence on the reality of the life of the body and a fierce joy in the pleasures of physical being. Nothing could be more opposed to Emerson's ideals than some of the tendencies and implications of Whitman's peoms, but they sprang from the same root.

In the light of all the foregoing facts the question naturally rises what did Emerson add to the system of ideas which had been the common belief of so many workers? He laid no claim to originality of material; indeed he did not think such originality possible. "If one require," he said in speaking of Shakespeare, "the originality which consists in weaving, like a spider, their own web from their bodies, no great men are original. Every master has found his material collected, and his power lay in his sympathy with his people and in his love of the materials he wrought in. What an economy of power!" Even this kind of originality, however, Emerson cannot wholly disclaim. To be sure, he was not the first to conceive the idea of the parallel between the physical and the spiritual laws, and he acknowledges fully the great help he gained in its development from the mystical, yet scientific works of Emanuel Swedenborg; but he showed very early an adoption of its principles in his own life, and his essays gave it a detailed exposition and helpful application. Moreover, by new combinations of the old ideas, he arrived at original conclusions, as for instance in the relation between the individual and the ultimate regeneration of the race.

But his final claim to greatness rests in himself more than in the substance of his teaching. He made a vast body of thoughts his own, welding them in the quiet processes of his mind into a faith rather than a system of thought; he adds thus to his words the irresistible power of his character. The very lessons he brought also took color from the mind through which they were passed. His optimism, for instance. was in great measure the product of his character. He was singularly free from human imperfections; someone has said of him that he scarcely knew the nature of temptation. He more than most men, therefore, could ignore the problems of evil, could rise above it and call it Nothing. He has been criticised for his optimism, and the criticism perhaps is just, if his teaching be taken as directed to society. But he always addressed the individual, and his disregard of evil enabled him to make his appeal positive and hopeful. It is at least an open question if this was not an element of strength in his teaching. It was certainly an element of originality. Finally he had an almost unique faculty of fitting his method to his purpose. He saw the universe as a symbol of its great Cause, and pondered upon the laws that run through mind and matter alike; but he could see as well the world full of men and women with daily problems to face. His task was to bring the truths he saw to the help of that world. The task was complicated because he was teaching individuals that they must not rely merely on teaching, but that every soul must arrive at its own truths. He met the situation by a body of thought that mingles the ideal and the practical in a way peculiarly his own, and that succeeds as but few teachings have succeeded in giving spiritual stimulus without imposing bonds. His work was based on a system of thought, but it forces no system on others.

One other element must be dwelt upon in gaining an understanding of what his words stand for; that is his relation to his country. It is not easy to give briefly the social, religious, and political condition of America as Emerson saw it in the early nineteenth century, but perhaps it may be described with sufficient exactness in the two words, dependence and materialism. He saw a nation cut loose from the demands that long years of Old World traditions had laid upon it, and able thus to offer an unparalleled chance of development to its individuals. Yet it had built up for itself a new tradition, quite as binding as the old, a tradition of deference to public opinion and the past. The people as a whole were bent chiefly on acquiring wealth; statesmen yielded to the demands of property; religious teachers were preaching a past creed instead of a present faith; and writers, teachers, and artists were building up in the New World a European culture. America was not a broad, forward-looking country with hopes and big plans for the future, but a mere creature of the past and of petty incentives. It is against this America that Emerson took his stand. He offered it aspirations, independence, and aims reaching beyond the present. It was a new ideal of freedom that he brought, real worship, rights for women, pure methods in politics and trade, a truly American art and literature, a broad educational policy, everything that could exalt the individual and give him the power of carrying out his higher will.

His teachings made their way slowly. His highest idealism could act, of course, only on the few; yet its influence must not be underestimated on that account. Gradually, however, the practical elements sifted themselves out of what was incomprehensible to the multitude, and worked themselves into the life and thought of his country. It is a tribute to Emerson rather than a depreciation of his work that many a common opinion of today can be traced to him or to the New England idealism of which he was the center.

## III. HOW TO STUDY THE ESSAYS.

In studying an essay of Emerson the aim should be to arrive at as complete a comprehension as possible of what the essay teaches, and to relate its thought to the body of teaching to which it belongs. A casual reading is of less help in the study of Emerson than is the case with most authors, though such a reading should be given. It must be followed, however, by a close study of the author's method and style and of his meaning in detail. Special questions on these points are offered on the following pages. They are, of course, only suggestions and must be varied to suit the class. Especially in the case of style and method should they be amplified. The peculiarities of Emerson's style have been the center of much criticism. They were in large measure the result of his desire to be suggestive and stimulating rather than authoritative. His method of composition followed out this theory. The thoughts that came to him were clothed in fitting sentence form and recorded in his Journal. When he composed a lecture, he grouped these recorded thoughts about some leading or central idea and gave them to the public, enriched with concrete illustrations. The essays were made from passages selected from the lectures, but the illustrations were mostly dropped and the language was condensed to only the most essential words. The result was essays of very peculiar structure. The thought is built up in sentences rather than in sentence or paragraph groups. This leads to many breaks, either real or apparent, which must be bridged from the reader's own thoughts. The lack of connection occurs between paragraphs, and between sentences in the paragraph as well. In some cases the sense runs easily from sentence to sentence until the break is reached; then the line of thought diverges into a new channel. The old thought is not always resumed. Often the break occurs because an idea is developed by the statement of facts assumed as true, where one might expect an explanation. The whole effect of the style is suggestive; it forces upon the reader the necessity of grasping a sentence completely, that is, of gaining from it what it contains and what it implies; every word must be studied.

When the reader has grasped the meaning of an essay in detail, he has gained in large measure its moral lessons. But the practice Emerson followed of showing first one phase and then another of his teaching, leaving the reader to balance contradictions and strike the medium of truth, creates often an impression of vagueness regarding the meaning of the essay as a whole. To supply the thread of logic the mind is unconsciously seeking, many methods are open. The suggestions and questions given for each essay separately on pages xxxvi to xxxix may prove helpful.

For the essay on *Manners,* (I) questions on method and style, (II) suggestions for the discussion of special passages, and (III) suggestions for the study of the teachings as a whole, are offered in the following pages. For the other essays, only suggestions for the study of the essay as a whole are given, but material suggestive as well as explanatory on special passages will be found in the *Notes* at the end of the volume.

## MANNERS

### I. Questions on Method and Style

**Page 2, line 27.** Note the break between this and the preceding paragraph. Supply the process of thought that would unite the two. Find other examples of broken transition between paragraphs.

**2, l. 31.** "The word gentleman" etc. Can the break between this sentence and the preceding be supplied?

**3, l. 13.** What is the relation of this sentence to what precedes and what follows?

**5, l. 10.** The figure of speech here is suggestive rather than explanatory. What does it suggest?

**6, l. 30.** What does this figure of speech suggest? Note whether other figures in the essay are explanatory or illustrative.

**7, l. 14.** In this paragraph select sentences that are mere statements where proof might be expected. Find other examples of the same method of development.

**8, l. 18.** Supply the statement omitted between this and the sentence in the preceding line.

**10, l. 32.** "A man," etc. What is the relation of this sentence to what precedes and what follows?

**11, l. 28.** "A gentleman," etc. Note the relation of this sentence to its context.

**15, l. 18.** "Conventional." Notice that the emphasis is laid on the derivation of the word. Are there other uses of this device?

**19, l. 4.** Contrast by reading aloud the rhythm of this paragraph with one from Webster or Hawthorne.

### II. Suggestions for the Discussion of Special Passages

**Page 3, line 25.** "Quantities" is used in a peculiar sense. Define it.

**5, l. 8.** "Memory" is here equivalent to established precedents which go down before a dominating personality. What quality of the gentleman is emphasized in this paragraph? Is it generally accepted as a quality of good manners? Why does Emerson emphasize it?

**6, l. 22.** Is this the method by which manners are actually revivified? The second part of the paragraph reminds one of the relations between Chesterfield and Dr. Johnson. See Macaulay's *Life of Johnson* and Boswell's *Johnson.*

**7, l. 14.** Does Emerson mean the "class of power" are gentlemen? Or the "polished circles"? Does this contradict the paragraph on page four in any sense?

**8, l. 10.** "The city," etc. What is the significance of this and the following sentences in the paragraph?

**8, l. 17.** Note how this paragraph emphasizes the fact that society, in the narrower sense of the word, is a natural product, and cannot therefore be set aside or forced.

**9, l. 20.** In what sense can this sentence and the following be accepted as true? Does the latter part of the paragraph tally with experience?

**9, l. 29.** Does society hate pretenders? Explain the next sentence. What is the leading idea of the paragraph? How are the last three sentences related to it? Is the paragraph consistent with *page* 15, *lines* 12-20. Can the two ideas be reconciled?

**11, l. 12.** Who are the "lesser gods"? The "loftier deities"? Is the last sentence in this paragraph idealistic or practical?

**11, l. 22.** In this paragraph note the emphasis again on the individual. Is physical, mental, or moral worth implied here as the basic idea of the gentleman? Note the quiet humor implied in "too great or too little."

**13, l. 21.** In what sense is "deference" explained by the paragraph. The aloofness described here is one very characteristic phase of Emerson's insistence on individuality. What sentence in the paragraph is the key to the secret of this attitude?

**15, l. 32.** What purpose does the qualifying nature of this paragraph serve in the general account of good manners? Note the moral turn given to the idea at the close. This is transitional to the next paragraph, which again leads into the following.

**17, l. 25.** How are the two ideas in this sentence opposed in thought? Fashion is symbolic of what? Evolved from what ideal? What disparity is there between Emerson's ideal of society and real society as pictured later in the paragraph? How does he reconcile them?

**19, l. 4.** Explain sentences two and three of this paragraph in their relation to the context. What is the underlying thought here? Is it only ideal? (Incidents such as took place when the Titanic went down must not be overlooked in answering this.)

**21, ll. 19-23.** Find illustrations in Scott and Shakespeare to test the point made.

**22, l. 3.** "I have seen an individual" etc., is a favorite method with Emerson of sketching an ideal. It is not always certain he had not someone in mind. This ideal person in Journal and essays alike he often calls Osman. See page 25, line 18.

**22, l. 15.** Note the opinion on woman's rights. By the term "musical nature" he signifies a natural fitness or sense of harmony that makes one receptive to the leading of Intuition.

Emerson was especially fortunate in his women friends. The first type of woman described may well be taken to reflect the personalities of Margaret Fuller, his aunt Mary Moody Emerson, and Sarah Ripley. In the second type there is a reminder of Ellen Tucker Emerson and of Elizabeth Hoar, whom he always called his sister as she was the betrothed wife of his brother Charles.

**24, l. 11.** This sentence is idealistic: Things are what our minds hold them to be; fashionable society melts to nothing, when the brave and the good say, "It is nothing unless it be good and useful."

**24, l. 15.** Note the humor and the irony at the close of this paragraph.

**25, l. 16.** What does he stigmatize in the term "national caution"?

**25, l. 30.** Does this paragraph settle upon any scheme for reorganizing imperfect society?

## III. Suggestions for the Study of the Essay as a Whole

The general thought in the essay on *Manners* takes two lines,—statements on society as a whole and statements on the gentleman. As Emerson presents, as usual, the ideal side by side with the actual, the whole essay may be grouped under four headings. A collection of some of the specific statements of the essay under these four groups will supply a partial tabulation that can be extended by the pupil.

A. The ideal of society.

1. Society is a self-constituted aristocracy, or fraternity of the best.
2. It makes its own whatever personal beauty or extraordinary native endowment anywhere appears.

B. Actual society:
   1. It is the average result of the character and faculties universally found in man.
   2. It is the spontaneous fruit of that class who have most vigor.

C. The ideal gentleman:
   1. The word is a homage to personal and incommunicable properties.
   2. The gentleman is a man of truth, lord of his own actions, expressing that lordship in his behavior; and the possessor of good nature and benevolence.

D. The gentleman as he sometimes exists:
   1. Frivolous and fantastic additions have got associated with the name.
   2. All sorts of gentlemen knock at the door.

The statements under each head will tend to group themselves around rather definite ideas, as for instance in A.:

*a.* The formation and constitution of society;
*b.* The relation of the man of force to society;
*c.* The qualities that gain entrance to society;
*d.* The true reason for the existence of society, and the advantages of a social code;
*e.* Society as a symbol of high spiritual facts.

Such questions as the following may serve to bring out the leading teachings more clearly.

1. Is Emerson too optimistic in his picture of actual society?

2. Does he intimate anywhere that he would forcibly abolish the faults of society? Does he hope for a slow reformation of society? Account for these facts. Discuss the bearing of the last paragraph upon them.

3. How do the statements under D of the outline emphasize his positive, optimistic method of teaching.

4. How many of the qualities assigned to the ideal gentleman may be traced back to Emerson's ideal of the individual?

5. Show in the whole characterization of the ideal gentleman that emphasis is laid on the moral sentiment (i. e. character as opposed to virtues), and hatred of moral cowardice. What to Emerson constitutes moral cowardice?

6. What remedy is offered to a person who feels aggrieved

at his position in society or at his exclusion from it? How is this idealistic?

7. What part do irony and humor play in the essay?

8. How does the essay stand related to the teaching of idealism? of evolution?

9. Discuss the optimism of the essay as a whole.

10. Show how Emerson's idea of the origin, constitution, and growth of society lays the responsibility for faults in it upon the individual. Is this ideal or practical? Why is it consistent with his whole philosophy?

## SELF-RELIANCE

The general teaching of this essay may be grouped around the following heads:

A. The ideal as it is set:
  - 1*a*. The self-reliant nation;
  - 1*b*. The lack of self-reliance as it reacts upon the nation;
  - 2*a*. The ideal of the self-reliant soul;
  - 2*b*. Hindrances to self-reliance in the individual.

B. Means of attaining the ideal:
  1. The relations between the self-reliant soul and universal Reason;
  2. The importance of the self-reliant soul as an agent of moral courage.

*Suggestive questions:* 1. To what nation is the appeal directed? 2. Why is lack of self-reliance moral cowardice? 3. How does the principle of Identity give unity to the whole essay? 4. Why does the last paragraph deserve to be called "the final trumpet call to faith"?

## COMPENSATION

The ethical value of this essay and its relation to Emerson's whole teaching may be brought out clearly by grouping its ideas after the following outline.

The working of the law of compensation.

A. In nature;

B. 1. On the wicked;

  2. On the good.

*Suggestive questions:* 1. What is crime in Emerson's view?

2. Can the inconsistency underlying the two divisions of B be reconciled? 3. What bearing has Emerson's optimism on this essay? 4. What is the unity of this essay?

## NATURE

The statements drawn from the portion on Efficient Nature might well be collected and grouped under the following general principles. In no essay in the book do we come closer to Emerson's own statement of his faith.

Parallels drawn between spiritual and physical laws:

A. Evolution or development;
 *a*. In external nature,
 *b*. In man.

B. Exaggeration;
 *a*. In external nature.
 *b*. In man.

C. Compensation;
 *a*. In nature,
 *b*. In man.

## FRIENDSHIP

There seems little necessity of analyzing this essay, as it has but one leading line of thought.

*Suggestive questions:* 1. What in detail are the ideal relationships of two individuals in a friendship? (Use " individual " in Emerson's meaning.) 2. Is there anything in his picture of friendship that undermines his constant insistence on a soul absolutely true to its own nature? 3. What type of man is capable of friendship in this large sense? 4. How does the doctrine of Identity underlie the thought of this essay? 5. What part do the emotions play in friendship as Emerson describes it? Is this wise or unwise? 6. Do Emerson's words of the advantage to the individual compensate for the aloofness this ideal involves? Defend your answer. 7. Emerson's idea of evolution in the physical world meant slow development or perfection. What bearing has the moral parallel of this law on his ideas of the ideal friendship?

# BIBLIOGRAPHICAL NOTE

(For a more complete bibliography see George W. Cooke's *A Bibliography of Ralph W. Emerson*, Boston and New York, 1908. There are bibliographical notes in the books by A. Ireland, R. Garnett, and M. Conway listed below.)

I. Helpful material for an historical background in the study of Emerson will be found in convenient compass in:—Barrett Wendell, *A Literary History of America*, Book II., Chapter 5, and Book V., Chapters 1, 4 and 5. John Nichol, *American Literature*, Edinburgh, 1882, Chapters 8 and 9. C. E. Richardson, *American Literature from* 1607 *to* 1885, Chapters 8 and 9. W. P. Trent, *A History of American Literature*, 1905, Chapter 6, to which is appended a bibliography of the Transcendental movement, etc.

II. TEXTS: The two standard editions of Emerson's works are:—The Riverside Edition, 12 volumes, and The Centenary Edition, 12 volumes.

The latter is annotated in an interesting, personal way by Edward Waldo Emerson.

III. BIOGRAPHY: Autobiographical material will be found in: *Journals of Ralph Waldo Emerson*, Boston, 1909, Edited by Edward Waldo Emerson and W. E. Forbes. *Correspondence of Carlyle and Emerson*, Boston, 1886, 2 volumes, Edited by C. E. Norton. *Correspondence of Emerson and John Sterling*, Boston, 1897, Edited by Edward Waldo Emerson. *Correspondence between Ralph Waldo Emerson and Herman Grimm*, Boston, 1903. Edited by F. W. Holls.

Five early and valuable lives of Emerson are:—J. E. Cabot, *A Memoir of Ralph Waldo Emerson*, Boston, 1887, 2 volumes. G. W. Cooke, *Ralph Waldo Emerson, His Life, Writings, and Philosophy*, Boston, 1881. Oliver Wendell Holmes, *Ralph Waldo Emerson*, Boston, 1885. (American Men of Letters Series.) Alexander Ireland, *In Memoriam—Ralph Waldo Emerson,*

London, 1882. This is of interest from its connection with Emerson's lecture tour in England. Richard Garnett, *Life of Ralph Waldo Emerson*, London, 1888. (Great Writers Series.)

Several books mentioned under I. have good biographical material.

Biographical material by relatives:—Edward Waldo Emerson, *Emerson in Concord*, Boston, 1889. This is of especial personal interest. Daniel Greene Haskins, *Ralph Waldo Emerson, his Maternal Ancestors*, Boston, 1887. This throws an interesting light on late colonial days in Boston, the personality of Madam Emerson, and Emerson's early childhood.

Other excellent biographies:—G. W. Woodberry, *Ralph Waldo Emerson*, New York, 1907. (English Men of Letters Series.) W. M. Payne, "Ralph Waldo Emerson" in *Leading American Essayists*, New York, 1910. This is very clear and concise. John Morley, "Emerson" in *Critical Miscellanies*, Vol. I, London, 1898. The life is short, and the appended criticism is brief but suggestive.

Books containing personal reminiscences of great interest with more or less direct biographical material and criticism:—Moncure D. Conway, *Emerson at Home and Abroad*, Boston, 1882. F. B. Sanborn, *The Genius and Character of Emerson*, Boston, 1885. This is a collection of lectures on Emerson given at the Concord School of Philosophy. Two of especial interest are by Miss E. P. Peabody and Mrs. Julia Ward Howe. C. J. Woodbury, *Talks with Ralph Waldo Emerson*, London, 1890. John Albee, *Remembrances of Emerson*, New York, 1901. James Russell Lowell, "Emerson the Lecturer" in *My Study Windows*, Boston, 1871. A. Bronson Alcott, *Ralph Waldo Emerson, Philosopher and Seer*, Boston, 1888. George William Curtis, "Emerson" in *Literary and Social Essays*, New York, 1894. This is also found in Elbert Hubbard's *Little Journeys to the Homes of American Authors*. It contains a graphic account of Emerson's home, and some of the friends gathered there. E. P. Whipple, *Recollections of Eminent Men*, 1886, pp. 119-154. Herman Grimm, "Ralph Waldo Emerson" in *Essays on Literature*, translated by S. H. Adams, Boston, 1888.

IV. Criticism: The following estimates of the character, philosophy and writings of Emerson are cited as showing a wide variety of opinion:—John J. Chapman, *Emerson and Other Essays*, New York, 1898. James Russell Lowell, *Fable for Critics*.

E. P. Whipple "Emerson as Poet" in *American Literature and Other Papers,* Boston, 1899. W. C. Brownell "Emerson" in *American Prose Masters,* New York, 1909. Matthew Arnold, "Emerson" in *Discourses on America,* New York, 1906. Leslie Stephen, "Emerson" in *Studies of a Biographer,* Vol. 4, New York, 1898. Henry James, "Emerson" in *Partial Portraits,* London, 1888. P. E. More, "Emerson" in *Shelburne Essays, First Series,* New York, 1907.

V. Magazine Articles: Such varied treatment of Emerson is given in permanent book form that there is little need of turning to files of periodicals. Two interesting and helpful articles are:—*Emerson,* by Henry James, Sr. *Atlantic Monthly,* Dec. 1904 (Vol. 94); and *Emerson as Seer,* by C. W. Eliot, *Atlantic,* June, 1903 (Vol. 91).

## CHRONOLOGICAL TABLE

| Emerson. | Contemporary Literature. | History and Biography. |
|---|---|---|
| 1803. Emerson born. | | 1803. Louisiana Treaty. |
| | | 1804. Bonaparte made Emperor; Hawthorne born. |
| | 1805. Scott, *Lay of the Last Minstrel.* | 1807, Longfellow, Whittier born. |
| | 1808. Scott, *Marmion.* | |
| | 1809. Irving, *History of New York.* | 1809. Lincoln, Holmes, Poe, Tennyson, Darwin, Gladstone born. |
| 1811. Death of Emerson's father. | | |
| | 1812. Byron, *Childe Harold,* Cantos I, II, | 1812-14. War with England. |
| 1813. Boston Latin School. | | |
| 1814. Family in Concord. | 1814. Wordsworth, *The Excursion.* | |
| | 1815. Miss Austen, *Emma.* | 1815. Battle of Waterloo. |
| 1817. Entered Harvard. | 1817. Bryant, *Thanatopsis.* | |
| | 1819. Irving, *Sketch Book.* | 1819. Lowell, Ruskin born. |
| | 1820. Scott, *Ivanhoe;* Shelley, *Prometheus Unbound;* Keats, *Lamia and other Poems.* | 1820-21. Missouri Compromise. |
| 1821. Graduated from college. | 1821. Cooper, *The Spy.* | 1821. Greek revolt. |
| 1821-25. A teacher. | 1822. De Quincey, *Confessions.* | |
| 1823. *Goodby, Proud World,* written. | 1823. Lamb, *Essays of Elia.* | 1823. Proclamation of the Monroe Doctrine, Shelley died. |
| 1825. Entered Harvard Divinity School. | 1825. Carlyle, *Life of Schiller;* Macaulay, *Essay on Milton.* | 1824. Byron died. |
| 1826. Illness; approbated to preach; first public sermon at Waltham. | 1826. Longfellow, first poems. | |
| 1826-27. In the South. | | 1827 Webster elected U. S. senator. |

CHRONOLOGICAL TABLE—*Continued.*

| Emerson. | Contemporary Literature. | History and Biography. |
|---|---|---|
| 1829. Ordained Assistant Pastor of Second Church, Boston; succeeded to pastorate; married Ellen Tucker. | | 1829. Catholic Emancipation in England. |
| | 1830. Tennyson, *Poems.* | 1830. Accession of William IV. in England; revolution in France. |
| 1831. Death of Ellen Tucker Emerson. | 1831. Poe, *Poems.* | |
| 1832. Resignation of his charge; voyage to Europe. | | 1832. Ordinance of Nullification in South Carolina; Reform Bill in England; Scott died. |
| 1833. Italy, France, England, and Scotland; return home. | 1833. Carlyle, *Sartor Resartus;* Browning, *Pauline.* | 1833. Anti-Slavery Society formed. |
| 1834. Four lectures in Boston; life in the Old Manse; *Nature,* written; death of Edward Emerson; correspondence with Carlyle begun. | 1834. Bancroft, *Colonization of the U.S.,* Vol. I. | 1834. Coleridge and Lamb died. |
| 1835. Marriage to Lydian Jackson; lectures on Biography and English Literature, Boston. | | |
| 1836. Death of Charles Emerson; twelve lectures in Boston; *Nature* published; *Sartor Resartus* edited. | 1836, Dickens, *Pickwick Papers;* Landor, *Pericles and Aspasia.* | |
| 1837. The American Scholar; first address on Slavery. | 1837. Prescott, *Ferdinand and Isabella;* Hawthorne, *Twice-Told Tales.* | 1837. Accession of Queen Victoria. |
| 1838. Divinity College address; *Michael Angelo.* | | |
| 1839. *Milton.* | | 1839. Chartist riots in England. |
| 1840. "The Dial," Vol. I., five prose pieces and three poems. | | 1840. Penny post established in England. |

CHRONOLOGICAL TABLE—*Continued.*

| Emerson. | Contemporary Literature. | History and Biography. |
|---|---|---|
| 1841. Death of eldest child; address on Nature; "The Dial," Vol. II., four contributions; *Essays, First Series.* | 1841. Carlyle, *Heroes and Hero-Worship.* | 1841. Brook Farm experiment. |
| 1843. Editor of "The Dial." | 1843. Webster, *Bunker Hill Speech;* Ruskin, *Modern Painters,* Vol. I. | |
| 1844. Eleven contributions to "The Dial"; *Essays, Second Series.* | | 1844. Morse telegraph. |
| 1845. Seven lectures on "Representative Men," Boston. | 1845. Poe, *The Raven.* | |
| | | 1846-48. Mexican War; 1846. Repeal of the English Corn Laws. |
| 1847. *May Day and Other Poems;* lecture course in Manchester, England. | 1847. Thackeray, *Vanity Fair.* | |
| 1848. Lecture courses in England and Scotland; visit to Paris. | 1848. Lowell, *Bigelow Papers;* Macaulay, *History of England,* Vols, I, II. Mill, *Principles of Political Economy.* | 1848. Gold discovered in California; revolution in France. |
| 1849. *Nature, Addresses and Lectures.* | | 1849. Poe died. |
| 1850. First lectures west of the Mississippi; *Representative Men.* | 1850. Hawthorne, *The Scarlet Letter;* Kingsley, *Alton Locke.* | 1850. Fugitive Slave Act; Webster's speech on the question; Wordsworth died. |
| 1851. Address on the Fugitive Slave Law. | | |
| 1852. *Memoirs of Margaret Fuller* (in collaboration). | 1852. Mrs. Stowe, *Uncle Tom's Cabin.* 1853. Matthew Arnold, *Poems.* | 1852. Clay, Webster died; Napoleon III. proclaimed Emperor. 1854-56. Crimean War. |
| 1855. Lectures on Slavery, Boston; Address at the Woman's Rights Convention, Boston. | 1855. Spencer, *Principles of Psychology;* Whitman, *Leaves of Grass.* | |

CHRONOLOGICAL TABLE—*Continued.*

| EMERSON. | CONTEMPORARY LITERATURE. | HISTORY AND BIOGRAPHY. |
|---|---|---|
| 1856. Speeches on the Assault on Mr. Sumner and on Kansas Relief; *English Traits*, *Samuel Hoar*. | | |
| 1857. *The Chartist's Complaint*. | | 1857. Dred Scott decision. |
| 1858. Address at Middlesex Agricultural Fair. | 1858. Holmes, *Autocrat;* Tennyson, *Idylls of the King*. | 1858. Lincoln-Douglas debate. |
| 1859. Burns Centenary speech. | 1859. Darwin, *Origin of Species;* Dickens, *Tale of Two Cities;* Fitz Gerald, *Rubáiyát;* Meredith, *Ordeal of Richard Feverel*. | 1859. John Brown's Raid. |
| 1860. Speeches on John Brown; *Conduct of Life*. | | 1860. War of Italian liberties. |
| 1860-70. Saturday Club. | | |
| 1861. *American Civilization*. | 1861. George Eliot, *Silas Marner;* Reade, *Cloister and the Hearth*. | 1861. Lincoln elected president; Civil War begun. |
| | 1863. Longfellow, *Tales of a Wayside Inn*. | 1863. Emancipation Proclamation; Battle of Gettysburg; Thackeray died. |
| | 1864. Newman, *Apologia pro sua Vita*. | 1864. Hawthorne died. |
| 1865. Memorial address on Lincoln; Harvard Commemoration Speech; *Thoreau's Letters* edited; *Living Age*. | 1865. Lowell, *Commemoration Ode;* Ruskin, *Sesame and Lilies*. | 1865. Close of Civil War; Assassination of Lincoln. |
| 1866. *Character*. | 1866. Whittier, *Snow Bound*. | 1866. Reform Bill in England. |
| 1867. *Progress of Culture*, Phi Beta Kappa address; LL.D. from Harvard; Overseer of Harvard; *Terminus; May-Day and other pieces*. | | |
| | 1868. Alcott, *Little Women*. | |

CHRONOLOGICAL TABLE—*Continued.*

| Emerson. | Contemporary Literature. | History and Biography. |
|---|---|---|
| | 1869. Browning, *The Ring and the Book.* Clemens, *Innocents Abroad;* Blackmore, *Lorna Doone.* | 1869. Opening of the Suez Canal. |
| 1870. Course in Philosophy at Harvard; *Society and Solitude.* | 1870. Huxley, *Lay Sermons and Addresses.* | 1870. Franco-Prussian War. |
| 1871. Repetition of lecture course at Harvard; trip to California. | 1871. Lowell, *My Study Windows.* | |
| 1872. Last of the annual lecture courses in Boston; trip to Europe. | | |
| | 1873. Arnold, *Literature and Dogma.* | |
| 1874. *Parnassus,* an anthology of English poems. | 1874. Mill, *Autobiography.* | |
| 1875. Nominated Lord Rector of Glasgow University. | | |
| 1876. Oration at the University of Virginia; *Select Poems; Letters and Social Aims.* | 1876. George Eliot, *Daniel Deronda.* | 1876. The Centennial. |
| | 1877. Morris, *Sigurd the Volsung;* Lanier, *Poems.* | |
| 1878. *Fortune of the Republic; The Sovereignty of Ethics.* | 1878. Henry James, *Daisy Miller;* Howells, *Lady of the Aroostook.* | 1878. Bryant died. |
| 1879. Founding of the Concord School of Philosophy; *The Preacher.* | 1879. Meredith, *The Egoist.* | |
| | | 1880. International Peace Association founded. |
| 1881. Address on Carlyle. | | 1881. Carlyle died. |
| 1882. *Superlatives;* death. | | 1882. Longfellow died. |

# MANNERS

"How near to good is what is fair!
Which we no sooner see,
But with the lines and outward air
Our senses taken be."

"Again yourselves compose,
And now put all the aptness on
Of Figure, that Proportion
Or Color can disclose;
That if those silent arts were lost,
Design and Picture, they might boast
From you a newer ground,
Instructed by the heightening sense
Of dignity and reverence
In their true motions found."

BEN JONSON.

HALF the world, it is said, knows not how the other half live. Our Exploring Expedition saw the Feejee islanders getting their dinner off human bones; and they are said to eat their own wives and children. The husbandry of the modern inhabitants of Gournou (west of old Thebes) is philosophical to a fault. To set up their housekeeping nothing is requisite but two or three earthen pots, a stone to grind meal, and a mat which is the bed. The house, namely a tomb, is ready without rent or taxes. No rain can pass through the roof, and there is no door, for there is no want of one, as there is nothing to lose. If the house do not please them, they walk out and enter another, as there are several hundreds at their command. "It is somewhat singular," adds Belzoni, to whom we owe this account, "to talk of happiness among people who live in sepulchres, among the corpses and rags of an ancient nation which they know nothing of." In the deserts of Borgoo the rock-Tibboos still dwell in caves, like cliff-swallows, and the language of these negroes is compared by their neighbors to the shrieking of bats and to the whistling of birds. Again, the Bornoos have no proper names; individuals are called after their height, thickness, or other accidental quality, and have nicknames merely. But the salt, the dates, the ivory, and the gold, for which these horrible regions are visited, find their way into countries where the purchaser and consumer can hardly be ranked in one race with these cannibals and man-stealers; countries where man serves himself with metals, wood, stone, glass, gum, cotton, silk and wool; honors himself with architecture; writes laws, and contrives to execute his will through the hands of many nations; and, especially, establishes a select society, running through all the countries of intelligent men, a self-constituted aristocracy, or fraternity of the best, which, without written law or exact usage of any kind, perpetuates itself, colonizes every new-planted island, and adopts and makes its own whatever personal beauty or extraordinary native endowment anywhere appears.

What fact more conspicuous in modern history than the creation of the gentleman? Chivalry is that, and loyalty is that, and in English literature half the drama, and all the novels, from Sir Philip Sidney to Sir Walter Scott, paint this figure. The word *gentleman,* which, like the word *Christian,* must hereafter characterize the present and the few preceding centuries by the importance attached to it, is a homage to personal and incommunicable properties. Frivolous and fantastic additions have got associated with the name, but the steady interest of mankind in it must be attributed to the valuable properties which it designates. An element which unites all the most forcible persons of every country, makes them intelligible and agreeable to each other, and is somewhat so precise that it is at once felt if an individual lack the masonic sign,—cannot be any casual product, but must be an average result of the character and faculties universally found in men. It seems a certain permanent average; as the atmosphere is a permanent composition, whilst so many gases are combined only to be decompounded. *Comme il faut,* is the Frenchman's description of good society: *as we must be.* It is a spontaneous fruit of talents and feelings of precisely that class who have most vigor, who take the lead in the world of this hour, and though far from pure, far from constituting the gladdest and highest tone of human feeling, is as good as the whole society permits it to be. It is made of the spirit, more than of the talent of men, and is a compound result into which every great force enters as an ingredient, namely virtue, wit, beauty, wealth and power.

There is something equivocal in all the words in use to express the excellence of manners and social cultivation, because the quantities are fluxional, and the last effect is assumed by the senses as the cause. The word *gentleman* has not any correlative abstract to express the quality. *Gentility* is mean, and *gentilesse* is obsolete. But we must keep alive in the vernacular the distinction between *fashion,* a word of narrow and often sinister meaning, and the heroic character which *the gentleman* imports. The usual words, however, must be respected: they will be found to contain the root of the matter. The point of distinction in all this class of names, as courtesy, chivalry, fashion, and the like, is that the flower and fruit, not the grain of the tree, are contemplated. It is beauty which is the aim this time, and not worth. The result is now in question, although our words intimate well enough the popular feeling that the appearance supposes a substance. The gentleman is a man of truth, lord of his own actions, and expressing that lordship in his behavior; not in any manner dependent and servile, either on persons, or opinions, or possessions. Beyond this fact of truth and real force, the word denotes good-nature or benevolence: manhood first, and then gentleness. The popular notion certainly adds a condition of ease and fortune; but that is a natural result of personal force and love, that they should possess and dispense the goods of the world. In times of violence, every eminent person must fall in with many opportunities to approve his stoutness and worth; therefore every man's name that emerged at all from the mass in the feudal ages rattles in our ear like a flourish of trumpets. But personal force never goes out of fashion. That is still paramount to-day, and in the moving crowd of good society the men of valor and reality are known and rise to their natural place. The competition is transferred from war to politics and trade, but the personal force appears readily enough in these new arenas.

Power first, or no leading class. In politics and in trade, bruisers and pirates are of better promise than talkers and clerks. God knows that all sorts of gentlemen knock at the door; but whenever used in strictness and with any emphasis, the name will be found to point at original energy. It describes a man standing in his own right and working after untaught methods. In a good lord there must first be a good animal, at least to the extent of yielding the incomparable advantage of animal spirits. The ruling class must have more, but they must have these, giving in every company the sense of power, which makes things easy to be done which daunt the wise. The society of the energetic class, in their friendly and festive meetings, is full of courage and of attempts which intimidate the pale scholar. The courage which girls exhibit is like a battle of Lundy's Lane, or a sea-fight. The intellect relies on memory to make some supplies to face these extemporaneous squadrons. But memory is a base mendicant with basket and badge, in the presence of these sudden masters. The rulers of society must be up to the work of the world, and equal to their versatile office: men of the right Cæsarian pattern, who have great range of affinity. I am far from believing the timid maxim of Lord Falkland ("that for ceremony there must go two to it; since a bold fellow will go through the cunningest forms"), and am of opinion that the gentleman is the bold fellow whose forms are not to be broken through; and only that plenteous nature is rightful master which is the complement of whatever person it converses with. My gentleman gives the law where he is; he will outpray saints in chapel, outgeneral veterans in the field, and outshine all courtesy in the hall. He is good company for pirates and good with academicians; so that it is useless to fortify yourself against him; he has the private entrance to all minds, and I could as easily exclude myself, as him. The famous gentlemen of Asia and Europe have been of this strong type; Saladin, Sapor, the Cid, Julius Cæsar, Scipio, Alexander, Pericles, and the lordliest personages. They sat very carelessly in their chairs, and were too excellent themselves, to value any condition at a high rate.

A plentiful fortune is reckoned necessary, in the popular judgment, to the completion of this man of the world; and it is a material deputy which walks through the dance which the first has led. Money is not essential, but this wide affinity is, which transcends the habits of clique and caste, and makes itself felt by men of all classes. If the aristocrat is only valid in fashionable circles and not with truckmen, he will never be a leader in fashion; and if the man of the people cannot speak on equal terms with the gentleman, so that the gentleman shall perceive that he is already really of his own order, he is not to be feared. Diogenes, Socrates, and Epaminondas, are gentlemen of the best blood who have chosen the condition of poverty when that of wealth was equally open to them. I use these old names, but the men I speak of are my contemporaries. Fortune will not supply to every generation one of these well-appointed knights, but every collection of men furnishes some example of the class; and the politics of this country, and the trade of every town, are controlled by these hardy and irresponsible doers, who have invention to take the lead, and a broad sympathy which puts them in fellowship with crowds, and makes their action popular.

The manners of this class are observed and caught with devotion by men of taste. The association of these masters with each other and with men intelligent of their merits, is mutually agreeable and stimulating. The good forms, the happiest expressions of each, are repeated and adopted. By swift consent everything superfluous is dropped, everything graceful is renewed. Fine manners show themselves formidable to the uncultivated man. They are a subtler science of defence to parry and intimidate; but once matched by the skill of the other party, they drop the point of the sword,—points and fences disappear, and the youth finds himself in a more transparent atmosphere, wherein life is a less troublesome game, and not a misunderstanding rises between the players. Manners aim to facilitate life, to get rid of impediments and bring the man pure to energize. They aid our dealing and conversation as a railway aids travelling, by getting rid of all avoidable obstructions of the road and leaving nothing to be conquered but pure space. These forms very soon become fixed, and a fine sense of propriety is cultivated with the more heed that it becomes a badge of social and civil distinctions. Thus grows up Fashion, an equivocal semblance, the most puissant, the most fantastic and frivolous, the most feared and followed, and which morals and violence assault in vain.

There exists a strict relation between the class of power and the exclusive and polished circles. The last are always filled or filling from the first. The strong men usually give some allowance even to the petulances of fashion, for that affinity they find in it. Napoleon, child of the revolution, destroyer of the old noblesse, never ceased to court the Faubourg St. Germain; doubtless with the feeling that fashion is a homage to men of his stamp. Fashion, though in a strange way, represents all manly virtue. It is virtue gone to seed: it is a kind of posthumous honor. It does not often caress the great, but the children of the great: it is a hall of the Past. It usually sets its face against the great of this hour. Great men are not commonly in its halls; they are absent in the field: they are working, not triumphing. Fashion is made up of their children; of those who through the value and virtue of somebody, have acquired lustre to their name, marks of distinction, means of cultivation and generosity, and in their physical organization a certain health and excellence which secure to them, if not the highest power to work, yet high power to enjoy. The class of power, the working heroes, the Cortez, the Nelson, the Napoleon, see that this is the festivity and permanent celebration of such as they; that fashion is funded talent; is Mexico, Marengo and Trafalgar beaten out thin; that the brilliant names of fashion run back to just such busy names as their own, fifty or sixty years ago. They are the sowers, their sons shall be the reapers, and *their* sons, in the ordinary course of things, must yield the possession of the harvest to new competitors with keener eyes and stronger frames. The city is recruited from the country. In the year 1805, it is said, every legitimate monarch in Europe was imbecile. The city would have died out, rotted and exploded, long ago, but that it was reinforced from the fields. It is only country which came to town day before yesterday that is city and court to-day.

Aristocracy and fashion are certain inevitable results. These mutual selections are indestructible. If they provoke anger in the least favored class, and the excluded majority revenge themselves on the excluding minority by the strong hand and kill them, at once a new class finds itself at the top, as certainly as cream rises in a bowl of milk: and if the people should destroy class after class, until two men only were left, one of these would be the leader and would be involuntarily served and copied by the other. You may keep this minority out of sight and out of mind, but it is tenacious of life, and is one of the estates of the realm. I am the more struck with this tenacity, when I see its work. It respects the administration of such unimportant matters, that we should not look for any durability in its rule. We sometimes meet men under some strong moral influence, as a patriotic, a literary, a religious movement, and feel that the moral sentiment rules man and nature. We think all other distinctions and ties will be slight and fugitive, this of caste or fashion for example; yet come from year to year and see how permanent that is, in this Boston or New York life of man, where too it has not the least countenance from the law of the land. Not in Egypt or in India a firmer or more impassable line. Here are associations whose ties go over and under and through it, a meeting of merchants, a military corps, a college class, a fire-club, a professional association, a political, a religious convention;—the persons seem to draw inseparably near; yet, that assembly once dispersed, its members will not in the year meet again. Each returns to his degree in the scale of good society, porcelain remains porcelain, and earthen earthen. The objects of fashion may be frivolous, or fashion may be objectless, but the nature of this union and selection can be neither frivolous nor accidental. Each man's rank in that perfect graduation depends on some symmetry in his structure or some agreement in his structure to the symmetry of society. Its doors unbar instantaneously to a natural claim of their own kind. A natural gentleman finds his way in, and will keep the oldest patrician out who has lost his intrinsic rank. Fashion understands itself; good-breeding and personal superiority of whatever country readily fraternize with those of every other. The chiefs of savage tribes have distinguished themselves in London and Paris by the purity of their tournure.

To say what good of fashion we can, it rests on reality, and hates nothing so much as pretenders; to exclude and mystify pretenders and send them into everlasting 'Coventry,' is its delight. We contemn in turn every other gift of men of the world; but the habit even in little and the least matters of not appealing to any but our own sense of propriety, constitutes the foundation of all chivalry. There is almost no kind of self-reliance, so it be sane and proportioned, which fashion does not occasionally adopt and give it the freedom of its saloons. A sainted soul is always elegant, and, if it will, passes unchallenged into the most guarded ring. But so will Jock the teamster pass, in some crisis that brings him thither, and find favor, as long as his head is not giddy with the new circumstance, and the iron shoes do not wish to dance in waltzes and cotillons. For there is nothing settled in manners, but the laws of behavior yield to the energy of the individual. The maiden at her first ball, the countryman at a city dinner, believes that there is a ritual according to which every act and compliment must be performed, or the failing party must be cast out of this presence. Later they learn that good sense and character make their own forms every moment, and speak or abstain, take wine or refuse it, stay or go, sit in a chair or sprawl with children on the floor, or stand on their head, or what else soever, in a new and aboriginal way; and that strong will is always in fashion, let who will be unfashionable. All that fashion demands is composure and self-content. A circle of men perfectly well-bred would be a company of sensible persons in which every man's native manners and character appeared. If the fashionist have not this quality, he is nothing. We are such lovers of self-reliance that we excuse in a man many sins if he will show us a complete satisfaction in his position, which asks no leave to be, of mine or any man's good opinion. But any deference to some eminent man or woman of the world, forfeits all privilege of nobility. He is an underling: I have nothing to do with him; I will speak with his master. A man should not go where he cannot carry his whole sphere or society with him,—not bodily, the whole circle of his friends, but atmospherically. He should preserve in a new company the same attitude of mind and reality of relation which his daily associates draw him to, else he is shorn of his best beams, and will be an orphan in the merriest club. "If you could see Vich Ian Vohr with his tail on!—" But Vich Ian Vohr must always carry his belongings in some fashion, if not added as honor, then severed as disgrace.

There will always be in society certain persons who are mercuries of its approbation, and whose glance will at any time determine for the curious their standing in the world. These are the chamberlains of the lesser gods. Accept their coldness as an omen of grace with the loftier deities, and allow them all their privilege. They are clear in their office, nor could they be thus formidable without their own merits. But do not measure the importance of this class by their pretension, or imagine that a fop can be the dispenser of honor and shame. They pass also at their just rate; for how can they otherwise, in circles which exist as a sort of herald's office for the sifting of character?

As the first thing man requires of man is reality, so that appears in all the forms of society. We pointedly, and by name, introduce the parties to each other. Know you before all heaven and earth, that this is Andrew, and this is Gregory;—they look each other in the eye; they grasp each other's hand, to identify and signalize each other. It is a great satisfaction. A gentleman never dodges: his eyes look straight forward, and he assures the other party, first of all, that he has been met. For what is it that we seek, in so many visits and hospitalities? Is it your draperies, pictures and decorations? Or do we not insatiably ask, Was a man in the house? I may easily go into a great household where there is much substance, excellent provision for comfort, luxury and taste, and yet not encounter there any Amphitryon who shall subordinate these appendages. I may go into a cottage, and find a farmer who feels that he is the man I have come to see, and fronts me accordingly. It was therefore a very natural point of old feudal etiquette that a gentleman who received a visit, though it were of his sovereign, should not leave his roof, but should wait his arrival at the door of his house. No house, though it were the Tuileries or the Escurial, is good for anything without a master. And yet we are not often gratified by this hospitality. Everybody we know surrounds himself with a fine house, fine books, conservatory, gardens, equipage and all manner of toys, as screens to interpose between himself and his guest. Does it not seem as if man was of a very sly, elusive nature, and dreaded nothing so much as a full rencontre front to front with his fellow? It were unmerciful, I know, quite to abolish the use of these screens, which are of eminent convenience, whether the guest is too great or too little. We call together many friends who keep each other in play, or by luxuries and ornaments we amuse the young people, and guard our retirement. Or if perchance a searching realist comes to our gate, before whose eye we have no care to stand, then again we run to our curtain, and hide ourselves as Adam at the voice of the Lord God in the garden. Cardinal Caprara, the Pope's legate at Paris, defended himself from the glances of Napoleon by an immense pair of green spectacles. Napoleon remarked them, and speedily managed to rally them off: and yet Napoleon, in his turn, was not great enough, with eight hundred thousand troops at his back, to face a pair of freeborn eyes, but fenced himself with etiquette and within triple barriers of reserve; and, as all the world knows from Madame de Staël, was wont, when he found himself observed, to discharge his face of all expression. But emperors and rich men are by no means the most skilful masters of good manners. No rent-roll nor army-list can dignify skulking and dissimulation; and the first point of courtesy must always be truth, as really all the forms of good-breeding point that way.

I have just been reading, in Mr. Hazlitt's translation, Montaigne's account of his journey into Italy, and am struck with nothing more agreeably than the self-respecting fashions of the time. His arrival in each place, the arrival of a gentleman of France, is an event of some consequence. Wherever he goes he pays a visit to whatever prince or gentleman of note resides upon his road, as a duty to himself and to civilization. When he leaves any house in which he has lodged for a few weeks, he causes his arms to be painted and hung up as a perpetual sign to the house, as was the custom of gentlemen.

The complement of this graceful self-respect, and that of all the points of good-breeding I most require and insist upon, is deference. I like that every chair should be a throne, and hold a king. I prefer a tendency to stateliness to an excess of fellowship. Let the incommunicable objects of nature and the metaphysical isolation of man teach us independence. Let us not be too much acquainted. I would have a man enter his house through a hall filled with heroic and sacred sculptures, that he might not want the hint of tranquillity and self-poise. We should meet each morning as from foreign countries, and, spending the day together, should depart at night, as into foreign countries. In all things I would have the island of a man inviolate. Let us sit apart as the gods, talking from peak to peak all round Olympus. No degree of affection need invade this religion. This is myrrh and rosemary to keep the other sweet. Lovers should guard their strangeness. If they forgive too much, all slides into confusion and meanness. It is easy to push this deference to a Chinese etiquette; but coolness and absence of heat and haste indicate fine qualities. A gentleman makes no noise: a lady is serene. Proportionate is our disgust at those invaders who fill a studious house with blast and running, to secure some paltry convenience. Not less I dislike a low sympathy of each with his neighbor's needs. Must we have a good understanding with one another's palates? as foolish people who have lived long together know when each wants salt or sugar. I pray my companion, if he wishes for bread, to ask me for bread, and if he wishes for sassafras or arsenic, to ask me for them, and not to hold out his plate as if I knew already. Every natural function can be dignified by deliberation and privacy. Let us leave hurry to slaves. The compliments and ceremonies of our breeding should recall, however remotely, the grandeur of our destiny.

The flower of courtesy does not very well bide handling, but if we dare to open another leaf and explore what parts go to its conformation, we shall find also an intellectual quality. To the leaders of men, the brain as well as the flesh and the heart must furnish a proportion. Defect in manners is usually the defect of fine perceptions. Men are too coarsely made for the delicacy of beautiful carriage and customs. It is not quite sufficient to good-breeding, a union of kindness and independence. We imperatively require a perception of, and a homage to beauty in our companions. Other virtues are in request in the field and workyard, but a certain degree of taste is not to be spared in those we sit with. I could better eat with one who did not respect the truth or the laws than with a sloven and unpresentable person. Moral qualities rule the world, but at short distances the senses are despotic. The same discrimination of fit and fair runs out, if with less rigor, into all parts of life. The average spirit of the energetic class is good sense, acting under certain limitations and to certain ends. It entertains every natural gift. Social in its nature, it respects everything which tends to unite men. It delights in measure. The love of beauty is mainly the love of measure or proportion. The person who screams, or uses the superlative degree, or converses with heat, puts whole drawing-rooms to flight. If you wish to be loved, love measure. You must have genius or a prodigious usefulness if you will hide the want of measure. This perception comes in to polish and perfect the parts of the social instrument. Society will pardon much to genius and special gifts, but, being in its nature a convention, it loves what is conventional, or what belongs to coming together. That makes the good and bad of manners, namely what helps or hinders fellowship. For fashion is not good sense absolute, but relative; not good sense private, but good sense entertaining company. It hates corners and sharp points of character, hates quarrelsome, egotistical, solitary and gloomy people; hates whatever can interfere with total blending of parties; whilst it values all peculiarities as in the highest degree refreshing, which can consist with good fellowship. And besides the general infusion of wit to heighten civility, the direct splendor of intellectual power is ever welcome in fine society as the costliest addition to its rule and its credit.

The dry light must shine in to adorn our festival, but it must be tempered and shaded, or that will also offend. Accuracy is essential to beauty, and quick perceptions to politeness, but not too quick perceptions. One may be too punctual and too precise. He must leave the omniscience of business at the door, when he comes into the palace of beauty. Society loves creole natures and sleepy languishing manners, so that they cover sense, grace and good-will: the air of drowsy strength, which disarms criticism; perhaps because such a person seems to reserve himself for the best of the game, and not spend himself on surfaces; an ignoring eye, which does not see the annoyances, shifts and inconveniences that cloud the brow and smother the voice of the sensitive.

Therefore besides personal force and so much perception as constitutes unerring taste, society demands in its patrician class another element already intimated, which it significantly terms good-nature,—expressing all degrees of generosity, from the lowest willingness and faculty to oblige, up to the heights of magnanimity and love. Insight we must have, or we shall run against one another and miss the way to our food; but intellect is selfish and barren. The secret of success in society is a certain heartiness and sympathy. A man who is not happy in the company cannot find any word in his memory that will fit the occasion. All his information is a little impertinent. A man who is happy there, finds in every turn of the conversation equally lucky occasions for the introduction of that which he has to say. The favorities of society, and what it calls *whole souls,* are able men and of more spirit than wit, who have no uncomfortable egotism, but who exactly fill the hour and the company; contented and contenting, at a marriage or a funeral, a ball or a jury, a water-party or a shooting-match. England, which is rich in gentlemen, furnished, in the beginning of the present century, a good model of that genius which the world loves, in Mr. Fox, who added to his great abilities the most social disposition and real love of men. Parliamentary history has few better passages than the debate in which Burke and Fox separated in the House of Commons; when Fox urged on his old friend the claims of old friendship with such tenderness that the house was moved to tears. Another anecdote is so close to my matter, that I must hazard the story. A tradesman who had long dunned him for a note of three hundred guineas, found him one day counting gold, and demanded payment. "No," said Fox, "I owe this money to Sheridan; it is a debt of honor; if an accident should happen to me, he has nothing to show." "Then," said the creditor, "I change my debt into a debt of honor," and tore the note in pieces. Fox thanked the man for his confidence and paid him, saying, "his debt was of older standing, and Sheridan must wait." Lover of liberty, friend of the Hindoo, friend of the African slave, he possessed a great personal popularity; and Napoleon said of him on the occasion of his visit to Paris, in 1805, "Mr. Fox will always hold the first place in an assembly at the Tuileries."

We may easily seem ridiculous in our eulogy of courtesy, whenever we insist on benevolence as its foundation. The painted phantasm Fashion rises to cast a species of derision on what we say. But I will neither be driven from some allowance to Fashion as a symbolic institution, nor from the belief that love is the basis of courtesy. We must obtain *that,* if we can; but by all means we must affirm *this.* Life owes much of its spirit to these sharp contrasts. Fashion, which affects to be honor, is often, in all men's experience, only a ballroom code. Yet so long as it is the highest circle in the imagination of the best heads on the planet, there is something necessary and excellent in it; for it is not to be supposed that men have agreed to be the dupes of anything preposterous; and the respect which these mysteries inspire in the most rude and sylvan characters, and the curiosity with which details of high life are read, betray the universality of the love of cultivated manners. I know that a comic disparity would be felt, if we should enter the acknowledged 'first circles' and apply these terrific standards of justice, beauty and benefit to the individuals actually found there. Monarchs and heroes, sages and lovers, these gallants are not. Fashion has many classes and many rules of probation and admission, and not the best alone. There is not only the right of conquest, which genius pretends,—the individual demonstrating his natural aristocracy best of the best;—but less claims will pass for the time; for Fashion loves lions, and points like Circe to her horned company. This gentleman is this afternoon arrived from Denmark; and that is my Lord Ride, who came yesterday from Bagdat; here is Captain Friese, from Cape Turnagain; and Captain Symmes, from the interior of the earth; and Monsieur Jovaire, who came down this morning in a balloon; Mr. Hobnail, the reformer; and Reverend Jul Bat, who has converted the whole torrid zone in his Sunday school; and Signor Torre del Greco, who extinguished Vesuvius by pouring into it the Bay of Naples; Spahi, the Persian ambassador; and Tul Wil Shan, the exiled nabob of Nepaul, whose saddle is the new moon.—But these are monsters of one day, and to-morrow will be dismissed to their holes and dens; for in these rooms every chair is waited for. The artist, the scholar, and, in general, the clerisy, win their way up into these places and get represented here, somewhat on this footing of conquest. Another mode is to pass through all the degrees, spending a year and a day in St. Michael's Square, being steeped in Cologne water, and perfumed, and dined, and introduced, and properly grounded in all the biography and politics and anecdotes of the boudoirs.

Yet these fineries may have grace and wit. Let there be grotesque sculpture about the gates and offices of temples. Let the creed and commandments even have the saucy homage of parody. The forms of politeness universally express benevolence in superlative degrees. What if they are in the mouths of selfish men, and used as means of selfishness? What if the false gentleman almost bows the true out of the world? What if the false gentleman contrives so to address his companion as civilly to exclude all others from his discourse, and also to make them feel excluded? Real service will not lose its nobleness. All generosity is not merely French and sentimental; nor is it to be concealed that living blood and passion of kindness does at last distinguish God's gentleman from Fashion's. The epitaph of Sir Jenkin Grout is not wholly unintelligible to the present age: "Here lies Sir Jenkin Grout, who loved his friend and persuaded his enemy: what his mouth ate, his hands paid for: what his servants robbed, he restored: he never forgot his children; and whoso touched his finger, drew after it his whole body." Even the line of heroes is not utterly extinct. There is still ever some admirable person in plain clothes, standing on the wharf, who jumps in to rescue a drowning man; there is still some absurd inventor of charities; some guide and comforter of runaway slaves; some friend of Poland; some Philhellene; some fanatic who plants shade-trees for the second and third generation, and orchards when he is grown old; some well-concealed piety: some just man happy in an ill fame; some youth ashamed of the favors of fortune and impatiently casting them on other shoulders. And these are the centres of society, on which it returns for fresh impulses. These are the creators of Fashion, which is an attempt to organize beauty of behavior. The beautiful and the generous are, in the theory, the doctors and apostles of this church: Scipio, and the Cid, and Sir Philip Sidney, and Washington, and every pure and valiant heart who worshipped Beauty by word and by deed. The persons who constitute the natural aristocracy are not found in the actual aristocracy, or only on its edge; as the chemical energy of the spectrum is found to be greatest just outside of the spectrum. Yet that is the infirmity of the seneschals, who do not know their sovereign when he appears. The theory of society supposes the existence and sovereignty of these. It divines afar off their coming. It says with the elder gods,—

As Heaven and Earth are fairer far
Than Chaos and blank Darkness, though once chiefs;
And as we show beyond that Heaven and Earth
In form and shape compact and beautiful; . . .
So on our heels a fresh perfection treads,
A power more strong in beauty, born of us
And fated to excel us, as we pass
In glory that old Darkness . . . .
. . . For 't is the eternal law
That first in beauty shall be first in might.

Therefore, within the ethnical circle of good society there is a narrower and higher circle, concentration of its light, and flower of courtesy, to which there is always a tacit appeal of pride and reference, as to its inner and imperial court; the parliament of love and chivalry. And this is constituted of those persons in whom heroic dispositions are native; with the love of beauty, the delight in society, and the power to embellish the passing day. If the individuals who compose the purest circles of aristocracy in Europe, the guarded blood of centuries, should pass in review, in such manner as that we could at leisure and critically inspect their behavior, we might find no gentleman and no lady; for although excellent specimens of courtesy and high-breeding would gratify us in the assemblage, in the particulars we should detect offence. Because elegance comes of no breeding, but of birth. There must be romance of character, or the most fastidious exclusion of impertinencies will not avail. It must be genius which takes that direction: it must be not courteous, but courtesy. High behavior is as rare in fiction as it is in fact. Scott is praised for the fidelity with which he painted the demeanor and conversation of the superior classes. Certainly, kings and queens, nobles and great ladies, had some right to complain of the absurdity that had been put in their mouths before the days of Waverley; but neither does Scott's dialogue bear criticism. His lords brave each other in smart epigrammatic speeches, but the dialogue is in costume, and does not please on the second reading: it is not warm with life. In Shakespeare alone the speakers do not strut and bridle, the dialogue is easily great, and he adds to so many titles that of being the best-bred man in England and in Christendom. Once or twice in a lifetime we are permitted to enjoy the charm of noble manners, in the presence of a man or woman who have no bar in their nature, but whose character emanates freely in their word and gesture. A beautiful form is better than a beautiful face; a beautiful behavior is better than a beautiful form: it gives a higher pleasure than statues or pictures; it is the finest of the fine arts. A man is but a little thing in the midst of the objects of nature, yet, by the moral quality radiating from his countenance he may abolish all considerations of magnitude, and in his manners equal the majesty of the world. I have seen an individual whose manners, though wholly within the conventions of elegant society, were never learned there, but were original and commanding and held out protection and prosperity; one who did not need the aid of a court-suit, but carried the holiday in his eye; who exhilarated the fancy by flinging wide the doors of new modes of existence; who shook off the captivity of etiquette, with happy, spirited bearing, good-natured and free as Robin Hood; yet with the port of an emperor, if need be,—calm, serious and fit to stand the gaze of millions.

The open air and the fields, the street and public chambers are the places where Man executes his will; let him yield or divide the sceptre at the door of the house. Woman, with her instinct of behavior, instantly detects in man a love of trifles, any coldness or imbecility, or, in short, any want of that large, flowing and magnanimous deportment which is indispensable as an exterior in the hall. Our American institutions have been friendly to her, and at this moment I esteem it a chief felicity of this country, that it excels in women. A certain awkward consciousness of inferiority in the men may give rise to the new chivalry in behalf of Woman's Rights. Certainly let her be as much better placed in the laws and in social forms as the most zealous reformer can ask, but I confide so entirely in her inspiring and musical nature, that I believe only herself can show us how she shall be served. The wonderful generosity of her sentiments raises her at times into heroical and godlike regions, and verifies the pictures of Minerva, Juno, or Polymnia; and by the firmness with which she treads her upward path, she convinces the coarsest calculators that another road exists than that which their feet know. But besides those who make good in our imagination the place of muses and of Delphic Sibyls, are there not women who fill our vase with wine and roses to the brim, so that the wine runs over and fills the house with perfume; who inspire us with courtesy; who unloose our tongues and we speak; who anoint our eyes and we see? We say things we never thought to have said; for once, our walls of habitual reserve vanished and left us at large; we were children playing with children in a wide field of flowers. Steep us, we cried, in these influences, for days, for weeks, and we shall be sunny poets and will write out in many-colored words the romance that you are. Was it Hafiz or Firdousi that said of his Persian Lilla, She was an elemental force, and astonished me by her amount of life, when I saw her day after day radiating, every instant, redundant joy and grace on all around her? She was a solvent powerful to reconcile all heterogeneous persons into one society: like air or water, an element of such a great range of affinities that it combines readily with a thousand substances. Where she is present all others will be more than they are wont. She was a unit and whole, so that whatsoever she did, became her. She had too much sympathy and desire to please, than that you could say her manners were marked with dignity, yet no princess could surpass her clear and erect demeanor on each occasion. She did not study the Persian grammar, nor the books of the seven poets, but all the poems of the seven seemed to be written upon her. For though the bias of her nature was not to thought, but to sympathy, yet was she so perfect in her own nature as to meet intellectual persons by the fulness of her heart, warming them by her sentiments; believing, as she did, that by dealing nobly with all, all would show themselves noble.

I know that this Byzantine pile of chivalry or Fashion, which seems so fair and picturesque to those who look at the contemporary facts for science or for entertainment, is not equally pleasant to all spectators. The constitution of our society makes it a giant's castle to the ambitious youth who have not found their names enrolled in its Golden Book, and whom it has excluded from its coveted honors and privileges. They have yet to learn that its seeming grandeur is shadowy and relative: it is great by their allowance; its proudest gates will fly open at the approach of their courage and virtue. For the present distress, however, of those who are predisposed to suffer from the tyrannies of this caprice, there are easy remedies. To remove your residence a couple of miles, or at most four, will commonly relieve the most extreme susceptibility. For the advantages which fashion values are plants which thrive in very confined localities, in a few streets namely. Out of this precinct they go for nothing; are of no use in the farm, in the forest, in the market, in war, in the nuptial society, in the literary or scientific circle, at sea, in friendship, in the heaven of thought or virtue.

But we have lingered long enough in these painted courts. The worth of the thing signified must vindicate our taste for the emblem. Everything that is called fashion and courtesy humbles itself before the cause and fountain of honor, creator of titles and dignities, namely the heart of love. This is the royal blood, this the fire, which in all countries and contingencies, will work after its kind and conquer and expand all that approaches it. This gives new meanings to every fact.

This impoverishes the rich, suffering no grandeur but its own. What *is* rich? Are you rich enough to help anybody? to succor the unfashionable and the eccentric? rich enough to make the Canadian in his wagon, the itinerant with his consul's paper which commends him "To the charitable," the swarthy Italian with his few broken words of English, the lame pauper hunted by overseers from town to town, even the poor insane or besotted wreck of man or woman, feel the noble exception of your presence and your house from the general bleakness and stoniness; to make such feel that they were greeted with a voice which made them both remember and hope? What is vulgar but to refuse the claim on acute and conclusive reasons? What is gentle, but to allow it, and give their heart and yours one holiday from the national caution? Without the rich heart, wealth is an ugly beggar. The king of Schiraz could not afford to be so bountiful as the poor Osman who dwelt at his gate. Osman had a humanity so broad and deep that although his speech was so bold and free with the Koran as to disgust all the dervishes, yet was there never a poor outcast, eccentric, or insane man, some fool who had cut off his beard, or who had been mutilated under a vow, or had a pet madness in his brain, but fled at once to him; that great heart lay there so sunny and hospitable in the centre of the country, that it seemed as if the instinct of all sufferers drew them to his side. And the madness which he harbored he did not share. Is not this to be rich? this only to be rightly rich?

But I shall hear without pain that I play the courtier very ill, and talk of that which I do not well understand. It is easy to see that what is called by distinction society and fashion has good laws as well as bad, has much that is necessary, and much that is absurd.

Too good for banning, and too bad for blessing, it reminds us of a tradition of the pagan mythology, in any attempt to settle its character. 'I overheard Jove, one day,' said Silenus, 'talking of destroying the earth; he said it had failed; they were all rogues and vixens, who went from bad to worse, as fast as the days succeeded each other. Minerva said she hoped not; they were only ridiculous little creatures, with this odd circumstance, that they had a blur, or indeterminate aspect, seen far or seen near; if you called them bad, they would appear so; if you called them good, they would appear so; and there was no one person or action among them which would not puzzle her owl, much more all Olympus, to know whether it was fundamentally bad or good.'

# SELF-RELIANCE

Ne te quæsiveris extra.

Man is his own star; and the soul that can
Render an honest and a perfect man,
Commands all light, all influence, all fate;
Nothing to him falls early or too late.
Our acts our angels are, or good or ill,
Our fatal shadows that walk by us still.

*Epilogue to Beaumont and Fletcher's Honest Man's Fortune.*

---

Cast the bantling on the rocks,
Suckle him with the she-wolf's teat,
Wintered with the hawk and fox,
Power and speed be hands and feet.

I READ the other day some verses written by an eminent painter which were original and not conventional. Always the soul hears an admonition in such lines, let the subject be what it may. The sentiment they instil is of more value than any thought they may contain. To believe your own thought, to believe that what is true for you in your private heart is true for all men,—that is genius. Speak your latent conviction, and it shall be the universal sense; for always the inmost becomes the outmost—and our first thought is rendered back to us by the trumpets of the Last Judgment. Familiar as the voice of the mind is to each, the highest merit we ascribe to Moses, Plato, and Milton is that they set at naught books and traditions, and spoke not what men, but what they thought. A man should learn to detect and watch that gleam of light which flashes across his mind from within, more than the lustre of the firmament of bards and sages. Yet he dismisses without notice his thought, because it is his. In every work of genius we recognize our own rejected thoughts; they come back to us with a certain alienated majesty. Great works of art have no more affecting lesson for us than this. They teach us to abide by our spontaneous impression with good-humored inflexibility then most when the whole cry of voices is on the other side. Else to-morrow a stranger will say with masterly good sense precisely what we have thought and felt all the time, and we shall be forced to take with shame our own opinion from another.

There is a time in every man's education when he arrives at the conviction that envy is ignorance; that imitation is suicide; that he must take himself for better for worse as his portion; that though the wide universe is full of good, no kernel of nourishing corn can come to him but through his toil bestowed on that plot of ground which is given to him to till. The power which resides in him is new in nature, and none but he knows what that is which he can do, nor does he know until he has tried. Not for nothing one face, one character, one fact, makes much impression on him, and another none. It is not without preestablished harmony, this sculpture in the memory. The eye was placed where one ray should fall, that it might testify of that particular ray. Bravely let him speak the utmost syllable of his confession. We but half express ourselves, and are ashamed of that divine idea which each of us represents. It may be safely trusted as proportionate and of good issues, so it be faithfully imparted, but God will not have his work made manifest by cowards. It needs a divine man to exhibit anything divine. A man is relieved and gay when he has put his heart into his work and done his best; but what he has said or done otherwise shall give him no peace. It is a deliverance which does not deliver. In the attempt his genius deserts him; no muse befriends; no invention, no hope.

Trust thyself: every heart vibrates to that iron string. Accept the place the divine providence has found for you, the society of your contemporaries, the connexion of events. Great men have always done so, and confided themselves childlike to the genius of their age, betraying their perception that the Eternal was stirring at their heart, working through their hands, predominating in all their being. And we are now men, and must accept in the highest mind the same transcendent destiny; and not pinched in a corner, not cowards fleeing before a revolution, but redeemers and benefactors, pious aspirants to be noble clay, under the Almighty effort let us advance on Chaos and the Dark.

What pretty oracles nature yields us on this text in the face and behavior of children, babes, and even brutes. That divided and rebel mind, that distrust of a sentiment because our arithmetic has computed the strength and means opposed to our purpose, these have not. Their mind being whole, their eye is as yet unconquered, and when we look in their faces, we are disconcerted. Infancy conforms to nobody; all conform to it; so that one babe commonly makes four or five out of the adults who prattle and play to it. So God has armed youth and puberty and manhood no less with its own piquancy and charm, and made it enviable and gracious and its claims not to be put by, if it will stand by itself. Do not think the youth has no force, because he cannot speak to you and me. Hark! in the next room who spoke so clear and emphatic? It seems he knows how to speak to his contemporaries. Good Heaven! it is he! it is that very lump of bashfulness and phlegm which for weeks has done nothing but eat when you were by, and now rolls out these words like bell-strokes. It seems he knows how to speak to his contemporaries. Bashful or bold then, he will know how to make us seniors very unnecessary.

The nonchalance of boys who are sure of a dinner, and would disdain as much as a lord to do or say aught to conciliate one, is the healthy attitude of human nature. How is a boy the master of society; independent, irresponsible, looking out from his corner on such people and facts as pass by, he tries and sentences them on their merits, in the swift, summary way of boys, as good, bad, interesting, silly, eloquent, troublesome. He cumbers himself never about consequences, about interests; he gives an independent, genuine verdict. You must court him; he does not court you. But the man is as it were clapped into jail by his consciousness. As soon as he has once acted or spoken with éclat he is a committed person, watched by the sympathy or the hatred of hundreds, whose affections must now enter into his account. There is no Lethe for this. Ah, that he could pass again into his neutral, godlike independence! Who can thus lose all pledge, and, having observed, observe again from the same unaffected, unbiased, unbribable, unaffrighted innocence, must always be formidable, must always engage the poet's and the man's regards. Of such an immortal youth the force would be felt. He would utter opinions on all passing affairs, which being seen to be not private but necessary, would sink like darts into the ear of men and put them in fear.

These are the voices which we hear in solitude, but they grow faint and inaudible as we enter into the world.

Society everywhere is in conspiracy against the manhood of every one of its members. Society is a joint-stock company, in which the members agree, for the better securing of his bread to each shareholder, to surrender the liberty and culture of the eater. The virtue in most request is conformity. Self-reliance is its aversion. It loves not realities and creators, but names and customs.

Whoso would be a man, must be a nonconformist. He who would gather immortal palms must not be hindered by the name of goodness, but must explore if it be goodness. Nothing is at last sacred but the integrity of our own mind. Absolve you to yourself, and you shall have the suffrage of the world. I remember an answer which when quite young I was prompted to make to a valued adviser who was wont to importune me with the dear old doctrines of the church. On my saying, What have I to do with the sacredness of traditions, if I live wholly from within? my friend suggested,—"But these impulses may be from below, not from above." I replied, "They do not seem to me to be such; but if I am the devil's child, I will live then from the devil." No law can be sacred to me but that of my nature. Good and bad are but names very readily transferable to that or this; the only right is what is after my constitution; the only wrong what is against it. A man is to carry himself in the presence of all opposition as if every thing were titular and ephemeral but he. I am ashamed to think how easily we capitulate to badges and names, to large societies and dead institutions. Every decent and well-spoken individual affects and sways me more than is right. I ought to go upright and vital, and speak the rude truth in all ways. If malice and vanity wear the coat of philanthropy, shall that pass? If an angry bigot assumes this bountiful cause of Abolition, and comes to me with his last news from Barbadoes, why should I not say to him, "Go love thy infant; love thy wood-chopper; be good-natured and modest; have that grace; and never varnish your hard, uncharitable ambition with this incredible tenderness for black folk a thousand miles off. Thy love afar is spite at home." Rough and graceless would be such greeting, but truth is handsomer than the affectation of love. Your goodness must have some edge to it,—else it is none. The doctrine of hatred must be preached, as the counteraction of the doctrine of love, when that pules and whines. I shun father and mother and wife and brother when my genius calls me. I would write on the lintels of the door-post, *Whim*. I hope it is somewhat better than whim at last, but we cannot spend the day in explanation. Expect me not to show cause why I seek or why I exclude company. Then, again, do not tell me, as a good man did to-day, of my obligation to put all poor men in good situations. Are they *my* poor? I tell thee, thou foolish philanthropist, that I grudge the dollar, the dime, the cent I give to such men as do not belong to me and to whom I do not belong. There is a class of persons to whom by all spiritual affinity I am bought and sold; for them I will go to prison if need be; but your miscellaneous popular charities; the education at college of fools; the building of meeting-houses to the vain end to which many now stand; alms to sots, and the thousandfold Relief Societies;—though I confess with shame I sometimes succumb and give the dollar, it is a wicked dollar which by-and-by I shall have the manhood to withhold.

Virtues are, in the popular estimate, rather the exception than the rule. There is the man *and* his virtues. Men do what is called a good action, as some piece of courage or charity, much as they would pay a fine in expiation of daily non-appearance on parade. Their works are done as an apology or extenuation of their living in the world,—as invalids and the insane pay a high board. Their virtues are penances. I do not wish to expiate, but to live. My life is not an apology, but a life. It is for itself and not for a spectacle. I much prefer that it should be of a lower strain, so it be genuine and equal, than that it should be glittering and unsteady. I wish it to be sound and sweet, and not to need diet and bleeding. My life should be unique; it should be an alms, a battle, a conquest, a medicine. I ask primary evidence that you are a man, and refuse this appeal from the man to his actions. I know that for myself it makes no difference whether I do or forbear those actions which are reckoned excellent. I cannot consent to pay for a privilege where I have intrinsic right. Few and mean as my gifts may be, I actually am, and do not need for my own assurance or the assurance of my fellows any secondary testimony.

What I must do is all that concerns me; not what the people think. This rule, equally arduous in actual and in intellectual life, may serve for the whole distinction between greatness and meanness. It is the harder because you will always find those who think they know what is your duty better than you know it. It is easy in the world to live after the world's opinion; it is easy in solitude to live after our own; but the great man is he who in the midst of the crowd keeps with perfect sweetness the independence of solitude.

The objection to conforming to usages that have become dead to you is that it scatters your force. It loses your time and blurs the impression of your character. If you maintain a dead church, contribute to a dead Bible Society, vote with a great party either for the

Government or against it, spread your table like base housekeepers,—under all these screens I have difficulty to detect the precise man you are. And of course so much force is withdrawn from your proper life. But do your thing, and I shall know you. Do your work, and you shall reinforce yourself. A man must consider what a blindman's-buff is this game of conformity. If I know your sect I anticipate your argument. I hear a preacher announce for his text and topic the expediency of one of the institutions of his church. Do I not know beforehand that not possibly can he say a new and spontaneous word? Do I not know that with all this ostentation of examining the grounds of the institution he will do no such thing? Do I not know that he is pledged to himself not to look but at one side, the permitted side, not as a man, but as a parish minister? He is a retained attorney, and these airs of the bench are the emptiest affectation. Well, most men have bound their eyes with one or another handkerchief, and attached themselves to some one of these communities of opinion. This conformity makes them not false in a few particulars, authors of a few lies, but false in all particulars. Their every truth is not quite true. Their two is not the real two, their four not the real four; so that every word they say chagrins us and we know not where to begin to set them right. Meantime nature is not slow to equip us in the prison-uniform of the party to which we adhere. We come to wear one cut of face and figure, and acquire by degrees the gentlest asinine expression. There is a mortifying experience in particular, which does not fail to wreak itself also in the general history; I mean 'the foolish face of praise,' the forced smile which we put on in company where we do not feel at ease, in answer to conversation which does not interest us. The muscles, not spontaneously moved but moved by a low usurping wilfulness, grow tight about the outline of the face, and make the most disagreeable sensation; a sensation of rebuke and warning which no brave young man will suffer twice.

For non-conformity the world whips you with its displeasure. And therefore a man must know how to estimate a sour face. The bystanders look askance on him in the public street or in the friend's parlor. If this aversation had its origin in contempt and resistance like his own he might well go home with a sad countenance; but the sour faces of the multitude, like their sweet faces, have no deep cause—disguise no god, but are put on and off as the wind blows and a newspaper directs. Yet is the discontent of the multitude more formidable than that of the senate and the college. It is easy enough for a firm man who knows the world to brook the rage of the cultivated classes. Their rage is decorous and prudent, for they are timid, as being very vulnerable themselves. But when to their feminine rage the indignation of the people is added, when the ignorant and the poor are aroused, when the unintelligent brute force that lies at the bottom of society is made to growl and mow, it needs the habit of magnanimity and religion to treat it godlike as a trifle of no concernment.

The other terror that scares us from self-trust is our consistency; a reverence for our past act or word because the eyes of others have no other data for computing our orbit than our past acts, and we are loath to disappoint them.

But why should you keep your head over your shoulder? Why drag about this monstrous corpse of your memory, lest you contradict somewhat you have stated in this or that public place? Suppose you should contradict yourself; what then? It seems to be a rule of wisdom never to rely on your memory alone, scarcely even in acts of pure memory, but to bring the past for judgment into the thousand-eyed present, and live ever in a new day. Trust your emotion. In your metaphysics you have denied personality to the Deity, yet when the devout motions of the soul come, yield to them heart and life, though they should clothe God with shape and color. Leave your theory, as Joseph his coat in the hand of the harlot, and flee.

A foolish consistency is the hobgoblin of little minds, adored by little statesmen and philosophers and divines. With consistency a great soul has simply nothing to do. He may as well concern himself with his shadow on the wall. Out upon your guarded lips! Sew them up with packthread, do. Else if you would be a man speak what you think to-day in words as hard as cannon balls, and to-morrow speak what to-morrow thinks in hard words again, though it contradict every thing you said to-day. Ah, then, exclaim the aged ladies, you shall be sure to be misunderstood! Misunderstood! It is a right fool's word. Is it so bad then to be misunderstood? Pythagoras was misunderstood, and Socrates, and Jesus, and Luther, and Copernicus, and Galileo, and Newton, and every pure and wise spirit that ever took flesh. To be great is to be misunderstood.

I suppose no man can violate his nature. All the sallies of his will are rounded in by the law of his being, as the inequalities of Andes and Himmaleh are insignificant in the curve of the sphere. Nor does it matter how you gauge and try him. A character is like an acrostic or Alexandrian stanza;—read it forward, backward, or across, it still spells the same thing. In this pleasing contrite wood-life which God allows me, let me record day by day my honest thought without prospect or retrospect, and, I cannot doubt, it will be found symmetrical, though I mean it not and see it not. My book should smell of pines and resound with the hum of insects. The swallow over my window should interweave that thread of straw he carries in his bill into my web also. We pass for what we are. Character teaches above our wills. Men imagine that they communicate their virtue or vice only by overt actions, and do not see that virtue or vice emit a breath every moment.

Fear never but you shall be consistent in whatever variety of actions, so they be each honest and natural in their hour. For of one will, the actions will be harmonious, however unlike they seem. These varieties are lost sight of when seen at a little distance, at a little height of thought. One tendency unites them all. The voyage of the best ship is a zigzag line of a hundred tacks. This is only microscopic criticism. See the line from a sufficient distance, and it straightens itself to the average tendency. Your genuine action will explain itself and will explain your other genuine actions. Your conformity explains nothing. Act singly, and what you have already done singly will justify you now. Greatness always appeals to the future. If I can be great enough now to do right and scorn eyes, I must have done so much right before as to defend me now. Be it how it will, do right now. Always scorn appearances and you always may. The force of character is cumulative. All the foregone days of virtue work their health into this. What makes the majesty of the heroes of the senate and the field, which so fills the imagination? The consciousness of a train of great days and victories behind. There they all stand and shed an united light on the advancing actor. He is attended as by a visible escort of angels to every man's eye. That is it which throws thunder into Chatham's voice, and dignity into Washington's port, and America into Adams's eye. Honor is venerable to us because it is no ephemeris. It is always ancient virtue. We worship it to-day because it is not of to-day. We love it and pay it homage because it is not a trap for our love and homage, but is self-dependent, self-derived, and therefore of an old immaculate pedigree, even if shown in a young person.

I hope in these days we have heard the last of conformity and consistency. Let the words be gazetted and ridiculous henceforward. Instead of the gong for dinner, let us hear a whistle from the Spartan fife. Let us bow and apologize never more. A great man is coming to eat at my house. I do not wish to please him: I wish that he should wish to please me. I will stand here for humanity; and though I would make it kind, I would make it true. Let us affront and reprimand the smooth mediocrity and squalid contentment of the times, and hurl in the face of custom and trade and office, the fact which is the upshot of all history, that there is a great responsible Thinker and Actor moving wherever moves a man; that a true man belongs to no other time or place, but is the centre of things. Where he is, there is nature. He measures you and all men and all events. You are constrained to accept his standard. Ordinarily, every body in society reminds us of somewhat else, or of some other person. Character, reality, reminds you of nothing else; it takes place of the whole creation. The man must be so much that he must make all circumstances indifferent—put all means into the shade. This all great men are and do. Every true man is a cause, a country, and an age; requires infinite spaces and numbers and time fully to accomplish his thought;—and posterity seem to follow his steps as a procession. A man Cæsar is born, and for ages after we have a Roman Empire. Christ is born, and millions of minds so grow and cleave to his genius that he is confounded with virtue and the possible of man. An institution is the lengthened shadow of one man; as, the Reformation, of Luther; Quakerism, of Fox; Methodism, of Wesley; Abolition, of Clarkson. Scipio, Milton called "the height of Rome;" and all history resolves itself very easily into the biography of a few stout and earnest persons.

Let a man then know his worth, and keep things under his feet. Let him not peep or steal, or skulk up and down with the air of a charity-boy, a bastard, or an interloper in the world which exists for him. But the man in the street, finding no worth in himself which corresponds to the force which built a tower or sculptured a marble god, feels poor when he looks on these. To him a palace, a statue, or a costly book have an alien and forbidding air, much like a gay equipage, and seem to say like that, 'Who are you, sir?' Yet they all are his, suitors for his notice, petitioners to his faculties that they will come out and take possession. The picture waits for my verdict; it is not to command me, but I am to settle its claim to praise. That popular fable of the sot who was picked up dead drunk in the street, carried to the duke's house, washed and dressed and laid in the duke's bed, and, on his waking, treated with all obsequious ceremony like the duke, and assured that he had been insane—owes its popularity to the fact that it symbolizes so well the state of man, who is in the world a sort of sot, but now and then wakes up, exercises his reason and finds himself a true prince.

Our reading is mendicant and sycophantic. In history our imagination makes fools of us, plays us false.

Kingdom and lordship, power and estate, are a gaudier vocabulary than private John and Edward in a small house and common day's work: but the things of life are the same to both: the sum total of both is the same. Why all this deference to Alfred and Scanderbeg and Gustavus? Suppose they were virtuous; did they wear out virtue? As great a stake depends on your private act to-day as followed their public and renowned steps. When private men shall act with original views, the lustre will be transferred from the actions of kings to those of gentlemen.

The world has indeed been instructed by its kings, who have so magnetized the eyes of nations. It has been taught by this colossal symbol the mutual reverence that is due from man to man. The joyful loyalty with which men have everywhere suffered the king, the noble, or the great proprietor to walk among them by a law of his own, make his own scale of men and things and reverse theirs, pay for benefits not with money but with honor, and represent the Law in his person, was the hieroglyphic by which they obscurely signified their consciousness of their own right and comeliness, the right of every man.

The magnetism which all original action exerts is explained when we inquire the reason of self-trust. Who is the Trustee? What is the aboriginal Self, on which a universal reliance may be grounded? What is the nature and power of that science-baffling star, without parallax, without calculable elements, which shoots a ray of beauty even into trivial and impure actions, if the least mark of independence appear? The inquiry leads us to that source, at once the essence of genius, the essence of virtue, and the essence of life, which we call Spontaneity or Instinct. We denote this primary wisdom as Intuition, whilst all later teachings are tuitions. In that deep force, the last fact behind which analysis cannot go, all things find their common origin. For the sense of being which in calm hours rises, we know not how, in the soul, is not diverse from things, from space, from light, from time, from man, but one with them and proceedeth obviously from the same source whence their life and being also proceedeth. We first share the life by which things exist and afterwards see them as appearances in nature and forget that we have shared their cause. Here is the fountain of action and the fountain of thought. Here are the lungs of that inspiration which giveth man wisdom, of that inspiration of man which cannot be denied without impiety and atheism. We lie in the lap of immense intelligence, which makes us organs of its activity and receivers of its truth. When we discern justice, when we discern truth, we do nothing of ourselves, but allow a passage to its beams. If we ask whence this comes, if we seek to pry into the soul that causes—all metaphysics, all philosophy is at fault. Its presence or its absence is all we can affirm. Every man discerns between the voluntary acts of his mind and his involuntary perceptions. And to his involuntary perceptions he knows a perfect respect is due. He may err in the expression of them, but he knows that these things are so, like day and night, not to be disputed. All my wilful actions and acquisitions are but roving;—the most trivial reverie, the faintest native emotion, are domestic and divine. Thoughtless people contradict as readily the statement of perceptions as of opinions, or rather much more readily; for they do not distinguish between perception and notion. They fancy that I choose to see this or that thing. But perception is not whimsical, but fatal. If I see a trait, my children will see it after me, and in course of time all mankind,—although it may chance that no one has seen it before me. For my perception of it is as much a fact as the sun.

The relations of the soul to the divine spirit are so pure that it is profane to seek to interpose helps. It must be that when God speaketh he should communicate, not one thing, but all things; should fill the world with his voice; should scatter forth light, nature, time, souls, from the centre of the present thought; and new date and new create the whole. Whenever a mind is simple and receives a divine wisdom, then old things pass away, —means, teachers, texts, temples fall; it lives now, and absorbs past and future into the present hour. All things are made sacred by relation to it,—one thing as much as another. All things are dissolved to their centre by their cause, and in the universal miracle petty and particular miracles disappear. This is and must be. If therefore a man claims to know and speak of God and carries you backward to the phraseology of some old mouldered nation in another country, in another world, believe him not. Is the acorn better than the oak which is its fulness and completion? Is the parent better than the child into whom he has cast his ripened being? Whence then this worship of the past? The centuries are conspirators against the sanity and majesty of the soul. Time and space are but physiological colors which the eye maketh, but the soul is light; where it is, is day; where it was, is night; and history is an impertinence and an injury if it be any thing more than a cheerful apologue or parable of my being and becoming.

Man is timid and apologetic; he is no longer upright; he dares not say "I think," "I am," but quotes some saint or sage. He is ashamed before the blade of grass or the blowing rose. These roses under my window make no reference to former roses or to better ones; they are for what they are; they exist with God to-day. There is no time to them. There is simply the rose; it is perfect in every moment of its existence. Before a leaf-bud has burst, its whole life acts; in the full-blown flower there is no more; in the leafless root there is no less. Its nature is satisfied and it satisfies nature in all moments alike. There is no time to it. But man postpones or remembers; he does not live in the present, but with reverted eye laments the past, or, heedless of the riches that surround him, stands on tiptoe to foresee the future. He cannot be happy and strong until he too lives with nature in the present, above time.

This should be plain enough. Yet see what strong intellects dare not yet hear God himself unless he speak the phraseology of I know not what David, or Jeremiah, or Paul. We shall not always set so great a price on a few texts, on a few lines. We are like children who repeat by rote the sentences of grandames and tutors, and, as they grow older, of the men of talents and character they chance to see,—painfully recollecting the exact words they spoke; afterwards, when they come into the point of view which those had who uttered these sayings, they understand them and are willing to let the words go; for at any time they can use words as good when occasion comes. So was it with us, so will it be, if we proceed. If we live truly, we shall see truly. It is as easy for the strong man to be strong, as it is for the weak to be weak. When we have new perception, we shall gladly disburthen the memory of its hoarded treasures as old rubbish. When a man lives with God, his voice shall be as sweet as the murmur of the brook and the rustle of the corn.

And now at last the highest truth on this subject remains unsaid; probably cannot be said; for all that we say is the far off remembering of the intuition. That thought, by what I can now nearest approach to say it, is this. When good is near you, when you have life in yourself,—it is not by any known or appointed way; you shall not discern the foot-prints of any other; you shall not see the face of man; you shall not hear any name;—the way, the thought, the good, shall be wholly strange and new. It shall exclude all other being. You take the way from man, not to man. All persons that ever existed are its fugitive ministers. There shall be no fear in it. Fear and hope are alike beneath it. It asks nothing. There is somewhat low even in hope. We are then in vision. There is nothing that can be called gratitude, nor properly joy. The soul is raised over passion. It seeth identity and eternal causation. It is a perceiving that Truth and Right are. Hence it becomes a Tranquillity out of the knowing that all things go well. Vast spaces of nature, the Atlantic Ocean, the South Sea; vast intervals of time, years, centuries, are of no account. This which I think and feel underlay that former state of life and circumstances, as it does underlie my present and will always all circumstances, and what is called life and what is called death.

Life only avails, not the having lived. Power ceases in the instant of repose; it resides in the moment of transition from a past to a new state, in the shooting of the gulf, in the darting to an aim. This one fact the world hates, that the soul *becomes;* for that forever degrades the past; turns all riches to poverty, all reputation to a shame; confounds the saint with the rogue, shoves Jesus and Judas equally aside. Why then do we prate of self-reliance? Inasmuch as the soul is present there will be power not confident but agent. To talk of reliance is a poor external way of speaking. Speak rather of that which relies because it works and is. Who has more soul than I masters me, though he should not raise his finger. Round him I must revolve by the gravitation of spirits. Who has less I rule with like facility. We fancy it rhetoric when we speak of eminent virtue. We do not yet see that virtue is Height, and that a man or a company of men, plastic and permeable to principles, by the law of nature must overpower and ride all cities, nations, kings, rich men, poets, who are not.

This is the ultimate fact which we so quickly reach on this, as on every topic, the resolution of all into the ever-blessed ONE. Virtue is the governor, the creator, the reality. All things real are so by so much virtue as they contain. Hardship, husbandry, hunting, whaling, war, eloquence, personal weight, are somewhat, and engage my respect as examples of the soul's presence and impure action. I see the same law working in nature for conservation and growth. The poise of a planet, the bended tree recovering itself from the strong wind, the vital resources of every animal and vegetable, are also demonstrations of the self-sufficing and therefore self-relying soul. All history, from its highest to its trivial passages, is the various record of this power.

Thus all concentrates; let us not rove; let us sit at home with the cause. Let us stun and astonish the intruding rabble of men and books and institutions by a simple declaration of the divine fact. Bid them take the shoes from off their feet, for God is here within. Let our simplicity judge them, and our docility to our own law demonstrate the poverty of nature and fortune beside our native riches.

But now we are a mob. Man does not stand in awe of man, nor is the soul admonished to stay at home, to put itself in communication with the internal ocean, but it goes abroad to beg a cup of water of the urns of men. We must go alone. Isolation must precede true society. I like the silent church before the service begins, better than any preaching. How far off, how cool, how chaste the persons look, begirt each one with a precinct or sanctuary. So let us always sit. Why should we assume the faults of our friend, or wife, or father, or child, because they sit around our hearth, or are said to have the same blood? All men have my blood and I have all men's. Not for that will I adopt their petulance or folly, even to the extent of being ashamed of it. But your isolation must not be mechanical, but spiritual, that is, must be elevation. At times the whole world seems to be in conspiracy to importune you with emphatic trifles. Friend, client, child, sickness, fear, want, charity, all knock at once at thy closet door and say, 'Come out unto us.'—Do not spill thy soul; do not all descend; keep thy state; stay at home in thine own heaven; come not for a moment into their facts, into their hubbub of conflicting appearances, but let in the light of thy law on their confusion. The power men possess to annoy me I give them by a weak curiosity. No man can come near me but through my act. "What we love that we have, but by desire we bereave ourselves of the love."

If we cannot at once rise to the sanctities of obedience and faith, let us at least resist our temptations, let us enter into the state of war and wake Thor and Woden, courage and constancy, in our Saxon breasts. This is to be done in our smooth times by speaking the truth. Check this lying hospitality and lying affection. Live no longer to the expectation of these deceived and deceiving people with whom we converse. Say to them, O father, O mother, O wife, O brother, O friend, I have lived with you after appearances hitherto. Henceforward I am the truth's. Be it known unto you that henceforward I obey no law less than the eternal law. I will have no covenants but proximities. I shall endeavor to nourish my parents, to support my family, to be the chaste husband of one wife,—but these relations I must fill after a new and unprecedented way. I appeal from your customs. I must be myself. I cannot break myself any longer for you, or you. If you can love me for what I am, we shall be happier. If you cannot, I will still seek to deserve that you should. I must be myself. I will not hide my tastes or aversions. I will so trust that what is deep is holy, that I will do strongly before the sun and moon whatever inly rejoices me and the heart appoints. If you are noble, I will love you; if you are not, I will not hurt you and myself by hypocritical attentions. If you are true, but not in the same truth with me, cleave to your companions; I will seek my own. I do this not selfishly but humbly and truly. It is alike your interest, and mine, and all men's, however long we have dwelt in lies, to live in truth. Does this sound harsh to-day? You will soon love what is dictated by your nature as well as mine, and if we follow the truth it will bring us out safe at last.—But so may you give these friends pain. Yes, but I cannot sell my liberty and my power, to save their sensibility. Besides, all persons have their moments of reason, when they look out into the region of absolute truth; then will they justify me and do the same thing.

The populace think that your rejection of popular standards is a rejection of all standard, and mere antinomianism; and the bold sensualist will use the name of philosophy to gild his crimes. But the law of consciousness abides. There are two confessionials, in one or the other of which we must be shriven. You may fulfil your round of duties by clearing yourself in the *direct,* or in the *reflex* way. Consider whether you have satisfied your relations to father, mother, cousin, neighbor, town, cat and dog; whether any of these can upbraid you. But I may also neglect this reflex standard and absolve me to myself. I have my own stern claims and perfect circle. It denies the name of duty to many offices that are called duties. But if I can discharge its debts it enables me to dispense with the popular code. If any one imagines that this law is lax, let him keep its commandment one day.

And truly it demands something godlike in him who has cast off the common motives of humanity and has ventured to trust himself for a task-master. High be his heart, faithful his will, clear his sight, that he may in good earnest be doctrine, society, law, to himself, that a simple purpose may be to him as strong as iron necessity is to others.

If any man consider the present aspects of what is called by distinction *society,* he will see the need of these ethics. The sinew and heart of man seem to be drawn out, and we are become timorous desponding whimperers. We are afraid of truth, afraid of fortune, afraid of death, and afraid of each other. Our age yields no great and perfect persons. We want men and women who shall renovate life and our social state, but we see that most natures are insolvent, cannot satisfy their own wants, have an ambition out of all proportion to their practical force, and so do lean and beg day and night continually. Our housekeeping is mendicant, our arts, our occupations, our marriages, our religion we have not chosen, but society has chosen for us. We are parlor soldiers. The rugged battle of fate, where strength is born, we shun.

If our young men miscarry in their first enterprises they lose all heart. If the young merchant fails, men say he is *ruined*. If the finest genius studies at one of our colleges, and is not installed in an office within one year afterwards, in the cities or suburbs of Boston or New York, it seems to his friends and to himself that he is right in being disheartened and in complaining the rest of his life. A sturdy lad from New Hampshire or Vermont, who in turn tries all the professions, who *teams it, farms it, peddles*, keeps a school, preaches, edits a newspaper, goes to Congress, buys a township, and so forth, in successive years, and always like a cat falls on his feet, is worth a hundred of these city dolls. He walks abreast with his days and feels no shame in not 'studying a profession,' for he does not postpone his life, but lives already. He has not one chance, but a hundred chances. Let a stoic arise who shall reveal the resources of man and tell men they are not leaning willows, but can and must detach themselves; that with the exercise of self-trust, new powers shall appear; that a man is the word made flesh, born to shed healing to the nations; that he should be ashamed of our compassion; and that the moment he acts from himself, tossing the laws, the books, idolatries and customs out of the window, we pity him no more but thank and revere him;—and that teacher shall restore the life of man to splendor and make his name dear to all History.

It is easy to see that a greater self-reliance—a new respect for the divinity in man—must work a revolution in all the offices and relations of men; in their religion; in their education; in their pursuits; their modes of living; their association; in their property; in their speculative views.

1. In what prayers do men allow themselves! That which they call a holy office is not so much as brave and manly. Prayer looks abroad and asks for some foreign

addition to come through some foreign virtue, and loses itself in endless mazes of natural and supernatural, and mediatorial and miraculous. Prayer that craves a particular commodity—anything less than all good, is vicious. Prayer is the contemplation of the facts of life from the highest point of view. It is the soliloquy of a beholding and jubilant soul. It is the spirit of God pronouncing his works good. But prayer as a means to effect a private end is theft and meanness. It supposes dualism and not unity in nature and consciousness. As soon as the man is at one with God, he will not beg. He will then see prayer in all action. The prayer of the farmer kneeling in his field to weed it, the prayer of the rower kneeling with the stroke of his oar, are true prayers heard throughout nature, though for cheap ends. Caratach, in Fletcher's Bonduca, when admonished to inquire the mind of the god Audate, replies,

> His hidden meaning lies in our endeavors;
> Our valors are our best gods.

Another sort of false prayers are our regrets. Discontent is the want of self-reliance: it is infirmity of will. Regret calamities if you can thereby help the sufferer; if not, attend your own work and already the evil begins to be repaired. Our sympathy is just as base. We come to them who weep foolishly and sit down and cry for company, instead of imparting to them truth and health in rough electric shocks, putting them once more in communication with the soul. The secret of fortune is joy in our hands. Welcome evermore to gods and men is the self-helping man. For him all doors are flung wide. Him all tongues greet, all honors crown, all eyes follow with desire. Our love goes out to him and embraces him because he did not need it. We solicitously and apologetically caress and celebrate him because he held on his way and scorned our disapprobation. The gods love him because men hated him. "To the persevering mortal," said Zoroaster, "the blessed Immortals are swift."

As men's prayers are a disease of the will, so are their creeds a disease of the intellect. They say with those foolish Israelites, "Let not God speak to us, lest we die. Speak thou, speak any man with us, and we will obey." Everywhere I am bereaved of meeting God in my brother, because he has shut his own temple doors and recites fables merely of his brother's, or his brother's brother's God. Every new mind is a new classification. If it prove a mind of uncommon activity and power, a Locke, a Lavoisier, a Hutton, a Bentham, a Spurzheim, it imposes its classification on other men, and lo! a new system. In proportion always to the depth of the thought, and so to the number of the objects it touches and brings within reach of the pupil, is his complacency. But chiefly is this apparent in creeds and churches, which are also classifications of some powerful mind acting on the great elemental thought of Duty and man's relation to the Highest. Such is Calvinism, Quakerism, Swedenborgianism. The pupil takes the same delight in subordinating every thing to the new terminology that a girl does who has just learned botany in seeing a new earth and new seasons thereby. It will happen for a time that the pupil will feel a real debt to the teacher—will find his intellectual power has grown by the study of his writings. This will continue until he has exhausted his master's mind. But in all unbalanced minds the classification is idolized, passes for the end and not for a speedily exhaustible means, so that the walls of the system blend to their eye in the remote horizon with the walls of the universe; the luminaries of heaven seem to them hung on the arch their master built. They cannot imagine how you aliens have any right to see—how you can see; 'It must be somehow that you stole the light from us.' They do not yet perceive that light, unsystematic, indomitable, will break into any cabin, even into theirs. Let them chirp awhile and call it their own. If they are honest and do well, presently their neat new pinfold will be too strait and low, will crack, will lean, will rot and vanish, and the immortal light, all young and joyful, million-orbed, million-colored, will beam over the universe as on the first morning.

2. It is for want of self-culture that the idol of Travelling, the idol of Italy, of England, of Egypt, remains for all educated Americans. They who made England, Italy, or Greece venerable in the imagination, did so not by rambling round creation as a moth round a lamp, but by sticking fast where they were, like an axis of the earth. In manly hours we feel that duty is our place and that the merry men of circumstance should follow as they may. The soul is no traveller: the wise man stays at home with the soul, and when his necessities, his duties, on any occasion call him from his house, or into foreign lands, he is at home still and is not gadding abroad from himself, and shall make men sensible by the expression of his countenânce that he goes, the missionary of wisdom and virtue, and visits cities and men like a sovereign and not like an interloper or a valet.

I have no churlish objection to the circumnavigation of the globe for the purposes of art, of study, and benevolence, so that the man is first domesticated, or does not go abroad with the hope of finding somewhat greater than he knows. He who travels to be amused or to get somewhat which he does not carry, travels away from himself, and grows old even in youth among old things. In Thebes, in Palmyra, his will and mind have become old and dilapidated as they. He carries ruins to ruins.

Travelling is a fool's paradise. We owe to our first journeys the discovery that place is nothing. At home I dream that at Naples, at Rome, I can be intoxicated with beauty and lose my sadness. I pack my trunk, embrace my friends, embark on the sea and at last wake up in Naples, and there beside me is the stern Fact, the sad self, unrelenting, identical, that I fled from. I seek the Vatican and the palaces. I affect to be intoxicated with sights and suggestions, but I am not intoxicated. My giant goes with me wherever I go.

3. But the rage of travelling is itself only a symptom of a deeper unsoundness affecting the whole intellectual action. The intellect is vagabond, and the universal system of education fosters restlessness. Our minds travel when our bodies are forced to stay at home. We imitate; and what is imitation but the travelling of the mind? Our houses are built with foreign taste; our shelves are garnished with foreign ornaments; our opinions, our tastes, our whole minds, lean, and follow the Past and the Distant, as the eyes of a maid follow her mistress. The soul created the arts wherever they have flourished. It was in his own mind that the artist sought his model. It was an application of his own thought to the thing to be done and the conditions to be observed. And why need we copy the Doric or the Gothic model? Beauty, convenience, grandeur of thought and quaint expression are as near to us as to any, and if the American artist will study with hope and love of the precise thing to be done by him, considering the climate, the soil, the length of the day, the wants of the people, the habit and form of the government, he will create a house in which all these

will find themselves fitted, and taste and sentiment will be satisfied also.

Insist on yourself; never imitate. Your own gift you can present every moment with the cumulative force of a whole life's cultivation; but of the adopted talent of another you have only an extemporaneous half possession. That which each can do best, none but his Maker can teach him. No man yet knows what it is, nor can, till that person has exhibited it. Where is the master who could have taught Shakspeare? Where is the master who could have instructed Franklin, or Washington, or Bacon, or Newton? Every great man is an unique. The Scipionism of Scipio is precisely that part he could not borrow. If anybody will tell me whom the great man imitates in the original crisis when he performs a great act, I will tell him who else than himself can teach him. Shakspeare will never be made by the study of Shakspeare. Do that which is assigned thee and thou canst not hope too much or dare too much. There is at this moment, there is for me an utterance bare and grand as that of the colossal chisel of Phidias, or trowel of the Egyptians, or the pen of Moses or Dante, but different from all these. Not possibly will the soul, all rich, all eloquent, with thousand-cloven tongue, deign to repeat itself; but if I can hear what these patriarchs say, surely I can reply to them in the same pitch of voice; for the ear and the tongue are two organs of one nature. Dwell up there in the simple and noble regions of thy life, obey thy heart and thou shalt reproduce the Foreworld again.

4. As our Religion, our Education, our Art look abroad, so does our spirit of society. All men plume themselves on the improvement of society, and no man improves.

Society never advances. It recedes as fast on one

side as it gains on the other. Its progress is only apparent like the workers of a treadmill. It undergoes continual changes; it is barbarous, it is civilized, it is christianized, it is rich, it is scientific; but this change is not amelioration. For every thing that is given something is taken. Society acquires new arts and loses old instincts. What a contrast between the well-clad, reading, writing, thinking American, with a watch, a pencil and a bill of exchange in his pocket, and the naked New Zealander, whose property is a club, a spear, a mat and an undivided twentieth of a shed to sleep under. But compare the health of the two men and you shall see that the aboriginal strength, the white man has lost. If the traveller tell us truly, strike the savage with a broad axe and in a day or two the flesh shall unite and heal as if you struck the blow into soft pitch, and the same blow shall send the white to his grave.

The civilized man has built a coach, but has lost the use of his feet. He is supported on crutches, but lacks so much support of muscle. He has got a fine Geneva watch, but he has lost his skill to tell the hour by the sun. A Greenwich nautical almanac he has, and so being sure of the information when he wants it, the man in the street does not know a star in the sky. The solstice he does not observe; the equinox he knows as little; and the whole bright calendar of the year is without a dial in his mind. His note-books impair his memory; his libraries overload his wit; the insurance-office increases the number of accidents; and it may be a question whether machinery does not encumber; whether we have not lost by refinement some energy, by a Christianity entrenched in establishments and forms some vigor of wild virtue. For every stoic was a stoic; but in Christendom where is the Christian?

There is no more deviation in the moral standard than in the standard of height or bulk. No greater men are now than ever were. A singular equality may be observed between the great men of the first and of the last ages; nor can all the science, art, religion, and philosophy of the nineteenth century avail to educate greater men than Plutarch's heroes, three or four and twenty centuries ago. Not in time is the race progressive. Phocion, Socrates, Anaxagoras, Diogenes, are great men, but they leave no class. He who is really of their class will not be called by their name, but be wholly his own man, and in his turn the founder of a sect. The arts and inventions of each period are only its costume and do not invigorate men. The harm of the improved machinery may compensate its good. Hudson and Behring accomplished so much in their fishing-boats as to astonish Parry and Franklin, whose equipment exhausted the resources of science and art. Galileo, with an opera-glass, discovered a more splendid series of facts than any one since. Columbus found the New World in an undecked boat. It is curious to see the periodical disuse and perishing of means and machinery which were introduced with loud laudation a few years or centuries before. The great genius returns to essential man. We reckoned the improvements of the art of war among the triumphs of science, and yet Napoleon conquered Europe by the Bivouac, which consisted of falling back on naked valor and disencumbering it of all aids. The Emperor held it impossible to make a perfect army, says Las Cases, "without abolishing our arms, magazines, commissaries and carriages, until, in imitation of the Roman custom, the soldier should receive his supply of corn, grind it in his hand-mill and bake his bread himself."

Society is a wave. The wave moves onward, but the

water of which it is composed does not. The same particle does not rise from the valley to the ridge. Its unity is only phenomenal. The persons who make up a nation to-day, die, and their experience with them.

And so the reliance on Property, including the reliance on governments which protect it, is the want of self-reliance. Men have looked away from themselves and at things so long that they have come to esteem what they call the soul's progress, namely, the religious, learned and civil institutions, as guards of property, and they deprecate assaults on these, because they feel them to be assaults on property. They measure their esteem of each other by what each has, and not by what each is. But a cultivated man becomes ashamed of his property, ashamed of what he has, out of new respect for his being. Especially he hates what he has if he see that it is accidental, came to him by inheritance, or gift, or crime; then he feels that it is not having; it does not belong to him, has no root in him, and merely lies there because no revolution or no robber takes it away. But that which a man is, does always by necessity acquire, and what the man acquires, is permanent and living property, which does not wait the beck of rulers, or mobs, or revolutions, or fire, or storm, or bankruptcies, but perpetually renews itself wherever the man is put. "Thy lot or portion of life," said the Caliph Ali, "is seeking after thee; therefore be at rest from seeking after it." Our dependence on these foreign goods leads us to our slavish respect for numbers. The political parties meet in numerous conventions; the greater the concourse and with each new uproar of announcement, The delegation from Essex! The Democrats from New Hampshire! The Whigs of Maine! the young patriot feels himself stronger than before by a new thousand of eyes and arms. In like manner the reformers summon conventions and vote and resolve in multitude. But not so, O friends! will the God deign to enter and inhabit you, but by a method precisely the reverse. It is only as a man puts off from himself all external support and stands alone that I see him to be strong and to prevail. He is weaker by every recruit to his banner. Is not a man better than a town? Ask nothing of men, and, in the endless mutation, thou only firm column must presently appear the upholder of all that surrounds thee. He who knows that power is in the soul, that he is weak only because he has looked for good out of him and elsewhere, and, so perceiving, throws himself unhesitatingly on his thought, instantly rights himself, stands in the erect position, commands his limbs, works miracles; just as a man who stands on his feet is stronger than a man who stands on his head.

So use all that is called Fortune. Most men gamble with her, and gain all, and lose all, as her wheel rolls. But do thou leave as unlawful these winnings, and deal with Cause and Effect, the chancellors of God. In the Will work and acquire, and thou hast chained the wheel of Chance, and shalt always drag her after thee. A political victory, a rise of rents, the recovery of your sick or the return of your absent friend, or some other quite external event raises your spirits, and you think good days are preparing for you. Do not believe it. It can never be so. Nothing can bring you peace but yourself. Nothing can bring you peace but the triumph of principles.

# COMPENSATION

EVER since I was a boy I have wished to write a discourse on Compensation; for it seemed to me when very young that on this subject Life was ahead of theology and the people knew more than the preachers taught. The documents too from which the doctrine is to be drawn, charmed my fancy by their endless variety, and lay always before me, even in sleep; for they are the tools in our hands, the bread in our basket, the transactions of the street, the farm and the dwelling-house; the greetings, the relations, the debts and credits, the influence of character, the nature and endowment of all men. It seemed to me also that in it might be shown men a ray of divinity, the present action of the Soul of this world, clean from all vestige of tradition; and so the heart of man might be bathed by an inundation of eternal love, conversing with that which he knows was always and always must be, because it really is now. It appeared moreover that if this doctrine could be stated in terms with any resemblance to those bright intuitions in which this truth is sometimes revealed to us, it would be a star in many dark hours and crooked passages in our journey, that would not suffer us to lose our way.

I was lately confirmed in these desires by hearing a sermon at church. The preacher, a man esteemed for his orthodoxy, unfolded in the ordinary manner the doctrine of the Last Judgment. He assumed that judgment is not executed in this world; that the wicked are successful; that the good are miserable; and then urged from reason and Scripture a compensation to be made to both parties in the next life. No offense appeared to be taken by the congregation at this doctrine. As far as I could observe when the meeting broke up they separated without remark on the sermon.

Yet what was the import of this teaching? What did the preacher mean by saying that the good are miserable in the present life? Was it that houses and lands, offices, wine, horses, dress, luxury, are had by unprincipled men, whilst the saints are poor and despised; and that a compensation is to be made to these last hereafter, by giving them the like gratifications another day,—bank-stock and doubloons, venison and champagne? This must be the compensation intended; for what else? Is it that they are to have leave to pray and praise? to love and serve men? Why, that they can do now. The legitimate inference the disciple would draw was, "We are to have *such* a good time as the sinners have now";—or, to push it to its extreme import,—"You sin now, we shall sin by-and-by: we would sin now, if we could; not being successful we expect our revenge to-morrow."

The fallacy lay in the immense concession that the bad are successful; that justice is not done now. The blindness of the preacher consisted in deferring to the base estimate of the market of what constitutes a manly success, instead of confronting and convicting the world from the truth; announcing the Presence of the Soul; the omnipotence of the Will; and so establishing the standard of good and ill, of success and falsehood, and summoning the dead to its present tribunal.

I find a similar base tone in the popular religious works of the day, and the same doctrines assumed by the literary men when occasionally they treat the related topics. I think that our popular theology has gained in decorum, and not in principle, over the superstitions it has displaced. But men are better than this theology. Their daily life gives it the lie. Every ingenuous and aspiring soul leaves the doctrine behind him in his own experience, and all men feel sometimes the falsehood which they cannot demonstrate. For men are wiser than they know. That which they hear in schools and pulpits without afterthought, if said in conversation would probably be questioned in silence. If a man dogmatize in a mixed company on Providence and the divine laws, he is answered by a silence which conveys well enough to an observer the dissatisfaction of the hearer, but his incapacity to make his own statement.

I shall attempt in this and the following chapter to record some facts that indicate the path of the law of Compensation; happy beyond my expectation if I shall truly draw the smallest arc of this circle.

POLARITY, or action and reaction, we meet in every part of nature; in darkness and light; in heat and cold; in the ebb and flow of waters; in male and female; in the inspiration and expiration of plants and animals; in the systole and diastole of the heart; in the undulations of fluids and of sound; in the centrifugal and centripetal gravity; in electricity, galvanism, and chemical affinity. Superinduce magnetism at one end of a needle, the opposite magnetism takes place at the other end. If the south attracts, the north repels. To empty here, you must condense there. An inevitable dualism bisects nature, so that each thing is a half, and suggests another thing to make it whole; as, spirit, matter; man, woman; subjective, objective; in, out; upper, under; motion, rest; yea, nay.

Whilst the world is thus dual, so is every one of its parts. The entire system of things gets represented in every particle. There is somewhat that resembles the ebb and flow of the sea, day and night, man and woman, in a single needle of the pine, in a kernel of corn, in each individual of every animal tribe. The reaction, so grand in the elements, is repeated within these small boundaries. For example, in the animal kingdom the physiologist has observed that no creatures are favorites, but a certain compensation balances every gift and every defect. A surplusage given to one part is paid out of a reduction from another part of the same creature. If the head and neck are enlarged, the trunk and extremities are cut short.

The theory of the mechanic forces is another example. What we gain in power is lost in time, and the converse. The periodic or compensating errors of the planets is another instance. The influences of climate and soil in political history are another. The cold climate invigorates. The barren soil does not breed fevers, crocodiles, tigers, or scorpions.

The same dualism underlies the nature and condition of man. Every excess causes a defect; every defect an excess. Every sweet hath its sour; every evil its good. Every faculty which is a receiver of pleasure has an equal penalty put on its abuse. It is to answer for its moderation with its life. For every grain of wit there is a grain of folly. For every thing you have missed, you have gained something else; and for every thing you gain, you lose something. If riches increase, they are increased that use them. If the gatherer gathers too much, nature takes out of the man what she puts into his chest; swells the estate, but kills the owner. Nature hates monopolies and exceptions. The waves of the sea do not more speedily seek a level from their loftiest tossing than the varieties of condition tend to equalize themselves. There is always some levelling circumstance that puts down the overbearing, the strong, the rich, the fortunate, substantially on the same ground with all others. Is a man too strong and fierce for society, and by temper and position a bad citizen,—a morose ruffian, with a dash of the pirate in him?—nature sends him a troop of pretty sons and daughters who are getting along in the dame's classes at the village school, and love and fear for them smooths his grim scowl to courtesy. Thus she contrives to intenerate the granite and felspar, takes the boar out and puts the lamb in and keeps her balance true.

The farmer imagines power and place are fine things. But the President has paid dear for his White House. It has commonly cost him all his peace, and the best of his manly attributes. To preserve for a short time so conspicuous an appearance before the world, he is content to eat dust before the real masters who stand erect behind the throne. Or do men desire the more substantial and permanent grandeur of genius? Neither has this an immunity. He who by force of will or of thought is great and overlooks thousands, has the responsibility of overlooking. With every influx of light comes new danger. Has he light? he must bear witness to the light, and always outrun that sympathy which gives him such keen satisfaction, by his fidelity to new revelations of the incessant soul. He must hate father and mother, wife and child. Has he all that the world loves and admires and covets?—he must cast behind him their admiration and afflict them by faithfulness to his truth and become a byword and a hissing.

This Law writes the laws of the cities and nations. It will not be baulked of its end in the smallest iota. It is in vain to build or plot or combine against it. Things refuse to be mismanaged long. *Res nolunt diu male administrari.* Though no checks to a new evil appear, the checks exist, and will appear. If the government is cruel, the governor's life is not safe. If you tax too high, the revenue will yield nothing. If you make a criminal code sanguinary, juries will not convict. Nothing arbitrary, nothing artificial can endure. The true life and satisfactions of man seem to elude the utmost rigors or felicities of condition and to establish themselves with great indifferency under all varieties of circumstance. Under all governments the influence of character remains the same,—in Turkey and New England about alike. Under the primeval despots of Egypt, history honestly confesses that man must have been as free as culture could make him.

These appearances indicate the fact that the universe is represented in every one of its particles. Every thing in nature contains all the powers of nature. Every thing is made of one hidden stuff; as the naturalist sees one type under every metamorphosis, and regards a horse as a running man, a fish as a swimming man, a bird as a flying man, a tree as a rooted man. Each new form repeats not only the main character of the type, but part for part all the details, all the aims, furtherances, hindrances, energies and whole system of every other. Every occupation, trade, art, transaction, is a compend of the world and a correlative of every other. Each one is an entire emblem of human life; of its good and ill, its trials, its enemies, its course and its end. And each one must somehow accommodate the whole man and recite all his destiny.

The world globes itself in a drop of dew. The microscope cannot find the animalcule which is less perfect for being little. Eyes, ears, taste, smell, motion, resistance, appetite, and organs of reproduction that take hold on eternity,—all find room to consist in the small creature. So do we put our life into every act. The true doctrine of omnipresence is that God reappears with all his parts in every moss and cobweb. The value of the universe contrives to throw itself into every point. If the good is there, so is the evil; if the affinity, so the repulsion; if the force, so the limitation.

Thus is the universe alive. All things are moral. That soul which within us is a sentiment, outside of us is a law. We feel its inspirations; out there in history we can see its fatal strength. It is almighty. All nature feels its grasp. "It is in the world, and the world was made by it." It is eternal but it enacts itself in time and space. Justice is not postponed. A perfect equity adjusts its balance in all parts of life. Οἱ κύβοι Διὸς ἀεὶ εὐπίπτουσι. The dice of God are always loaded. The world looks like a multiplication-table, or a mathematical equation, which, turn it how you will, balances itself. Take what figure you will, its exact value, nor more nor less, still returns to you. Every secret is told, every crime is punished, every virtue rewarded, every wrong redressed, in silence and certainty. What we call retribution is the universal necessity by which the whole appears wherever a part appears. If you see smoke, there must be fire. If you see a hand or limb, you know that the trunk to which it belongs is there behind.

Every act rewards itself, or in other words integrates itself, in a twofold manner: first in the thing, or in real nature; and secondly in the circumstance, or in apparent nature. Men call the circumstance the retribution. The casual retribution is in the thing and is seen by the soul. The retribution in the circumstance is seen by the understanding; it is inseparable from the thing, but is often spread over a long time and so does not become distinct until after many years. The specific stripes may follow late after the offence, but they follow because they accompany it. Crime and punishment grow out of one stem. Punishment is a fruit that unsuspected ripens within the flower of the pleasure which concealed it. Cause and effect, means and ends, seed and fruit, cannot be severed; for the effect already blooms in the cause, the end preëxists in the means, the fruit in the seed.

Whilst thus the world will be whole and refuses to be disparted, we seek to act partially, to sunder, to appropriate; for example,—to gratify the senses we sever the pleasure of the senses from the needs of the character. The ingenuity of man has been dedicated to the solution of one problem,—how to detach the sensual sweet, the sensual strong, the sensual bright, etc., from the moral sweet, the moral deep, the moral fair; that is, again, to contrive to cut clean off this upper surface so thin as to leave it bottomless; to get a *one end,* without an *other end.* The soul says, Eat; the body would feast. The soul says, The man and woman shall be one flesh and one soul; the body would join the flesh only. The soul says, Have dominion over all things to the ends of virtue; the body would have the power over things to its own ends.

The soul strives amain to live and work through all things. It would be the only fact. All things shall be added unto it,—power, pleasure, knowledge, beauty. The particular man aims to be somebody; to set up for himself; to truck and higgle for a private good; and, in particulars, to ride that he may ride; to dress that he may be dressed; to eat that he may eat; and to govern, that he may be seen. Men seek to be great; they would have offices, wealth, power, and fame. They think that to be great is to get only one side of nature,—the sweet, without the other side,—the bitter.

Steadily is this dividing and detaching counteracted. Up to this day it must be owned no projector has had the smallest success. The parted water reunites behind our hand. Pleasure is taken out of pleasant things, profit out of profitable things, power out of strong things, the moment we seek to separate them from the whole. We can no more halve things and get the sensual good, by itself, than we can get an inside that shall have no outside, or a light without a shadow. "Drive out nature with a fork, she comes running back."

Life invests itself with inevitable conditions, which the unwise seek to dodge, which one and another brags that he does not know, brags that they do not touch him;—but the brag is on his lips, the conditions are in his soul. If he escapes them in one part they attack him in another more vital part. If he has escaped them in form and in appearance, it is because he has resisted his life and fled from himself, and the retribution is so much death. So signal is the failure of all attempts to make this separation of the good from the tax, that the experiment would not be tried,—since to try it is to be mad,—but for the circumstance that when the disease began in the will, of rebellion and separation, the intellect is at once infected, so that the man ceases to see God whole in each object, but is able to see the sensual allurement of an object and not see the sensual hurt; he sees the mermaid's head but not the dragon's tail, and thinks he can cut off that which he would have from that which he would not have. "How secret art thou who dwellest in the highest heavens in silence, O thou only great God, sprinkling with an unwearied providence certain penal blindnesses upon such as have unbridled desires!"

The human soul is true to these facts in the painting of fable, of history, of law, of proverbs, of conversation. It finds a tongue in literature unawares. Thus the Greeks called Jupiter, Supreme Mind; but having traditionally ascribed to him many base actions, they involuntarily made amends to Reason by tying up the hands of so bad a god. He is made as helpless as a king of England. Prometheus knows one secret which Jove must bargain for; Minerva, another. He cannot get his own thunders; Minerva keeps the key of them:

> Of all the gods, I only know the keys
> That ope the solid doors within whose vaults
> His thunders sleep.

A plain confession of the in-working of the All and of its moral aim. The Indian mythology ends in the same ethics; and indeed it would seem impossible for any fable to be invented and get any currency which was not moral. Aurora forgot to ask youth for her lover, and so though Tithonus is immortal, he is old. Achilles is not quite invulnerable; for Thetis held him by the heel when she dipped him in the Styx and the sacred waters did not wash that part. Siegfried, in the Nibelungen, is not quite immortal, for a leaf fell on his back whilst he was bathing in the Dragon's blood, and that spot which it covered is mortal. And so it always is. There is a crack in every thing God has made. Always it would seem there is this vindictive circumstance stealing in at unawares even into the wild poesy in which the human fancy attempted to make bold holiday and to shake itself free of the old laws,—this back-stroke, this kick of the gun, certifying that the law is fatal; that in nature nothing can be given, all things are sold.

This is that ancient doctrine of Nemesis, who keeps

watch in the Universe and lets no offence go unchastised. The Furies, they said, are attendants on Justice, and if the sun in heaven should transgress his path they would punish him. The poets related that stone walls and iron swords and leathern thongs had an occult sympathy with the wrongs of their owners; that the belt which Ajax gave Hector dragged the Trojan hero over the field at the wheels of the car of Achilles, and the sword which Hector gave Ajax was that on whose point Ajax fell. They recorded that when the Thasians erected a statue to Theagenes, a victor in the games, one of his rivals went to it by night and endeavored to throw it down by repeated blows, until at last he moved it from its pedestal and was crushed to death beneath its fall.

This voice of fable has in it somewhat divine. It came from thought above the will of the writer. That is the best part of each writer which has nothing private in it; that is the best part of each which he does not know; that which flowed out of his constitution and not from his too active invention; that which in the study of a single artist you might not easily find, but in the study of many you would abstract as the spirit of them all. Phidias it is not, but the work of man in that early Hellenic world that I would know. The name and circumstance of Phidias, however convenient for history, embarrasses when we come to the highest criticism. We are to see that which man was tending to do in a given period, and was hindered, or, if you will, modified in doing, by the interfering volitions of Phidias, of Dante, of Shakspeare, the organ whereby man at the moment wrought.

Still more striking is the expression of this fact in the proverbs of all nations, which are always the literature of Reason, or the statements of an absolute truth without qualification. Proverbs, like the sacred books of each nation, are the sanctuary of the Intuitions. That which the droning world, chained to appearances, will not allow the realist to say in his own words, it will suffer him to say in proverbs without contradiction. And this law of laws, which the pulpit, the senate and the college deny, is hourly preached in all markets and all languages by flights of proverbs, whose teaching is as true and as omnipresent as that of birds and flies.

All things are double, one against another.—Tit for tat; an eye for an eye; a tooth for a tooth; blood for blood; measure for measure; love for love.—Give, and it shall be given you.—He that watereth shall be watered himself.—What will you have? quoth God; pay for it and take it.—Nothing venture, nothing have.—Thou shalt be paid exactly for what thou hast done, no more, no less.—Who doth not work shall not eat.—Harm watch, harm catch.—Curses always recoil on the head of him who imprecates them.—If you put a chain around the neck of a slave, the other end fastens itself around your own.—Bad counsel confounds the adviser.—The devil is an ass.

It is thus written, because it is thus in life. Our action is overmastered and characterized above our will by the laws of nature. We aim at a petty end quite aside from the public good, but our act arranges itself by irresistible magnetism in a line with the poles of the world.

A man cannot speak but he judges himself. With his will or against his will he draws his portrait to the eye of his companions by every word. Every opinion reacts on him who utters it. It is a threadball thrown at a mark, but the other end remains in the thrower's bag. Or rather, it is a harpoon thrown at the whale, unwinding, as it flies, a coil of cord in the boat, and, if the harpoon is not good, or not well thrown, it will go nigh to cut the steersman in twain or to sink the boat.

You cannot do wrong without suffering wrong. "No man had ever a point of pride that was not injurious to him," said Burke. The exclusive in fashionable life does not see that he excludes himself from enjoyment, in the attempt to appropriate it. The exclusionist in religion does not see that he shuts the door of heaven on himself, in striving to shut out others. Treat men as pawns and ninepins, and you shall suffer as well as they. If you leave out their heart, you shall lose your own. The senses would make things of all persons; of women, of children, of the poor. The vulgar proverb, "I will get it from his purse or get it from his skin," is sound philosophy.

All infractions of love and equity in our social relations are speedily punished. They are punished by Fear. Whilst I stand in simple relations to my fellow-man, I have no displeasure in meeting him. We meet as water meets water, or as two currents of air mix, with perfect diffusion and interpenetration of nature. But as soon as there is any departure from simplicity and attempt at halfness, or good for me that is not good for him, my neighbor feels the wrong; he shrinks from me as far as I have shrunk from him; his eyes no longer seek mine; there is war between us; there is hate in him and fear in me.

All the old abuses in society, the great and universal and the petty and particular, all unjust accumulations of property and power, are avenged in the same manner. Fear is an instructor of great sagacity and the herald of all revolutions. One thing he always teaches, that there is rottenness where he appears. He is a carrion crow, and though you see not well what he hovers for, there is death somewhere. Our property is timid, our laws are timid, our cultivated classes are timid. Fear for ages has boded and mowed and gibbered over government and property. That obscene bird is not there for nothing. He indicates great wrongs which must be revised.

Of the like nature is that expectation of change which instantly follows the suspension of our voluntary activity. The terror of cloudless noon, the emerald of Polycrates, the awe of prosperity, the instinct which leads every generous soul to impose on itself tasks of a noble asceticism and vicarious virtue, are the tremblings of the balance of justice through the heart and mind of man.

Experienced men of the world know very well that it is best to pay scot and lot as they go along, and that a man often pays dear for a small frugality. The borrower runs in his own debt. Has a man gained any thing who has received a hundred favors and rendered none? Has he gained by borrowing, through indolence or cunning, his neighbor's wares, or horses, or money? There arises on the deed the instant acknowledgment of benefit on the one part and of debt on the other; that is, of superiority and inferiority. The transaction remains in the memory of himself and his neighbor; and every new transaction alters according to its nature their relation to each other. He may soon come to see that he had better have broken his own bones than to have ridden in his neighbor's coach, and that "the highest price he can pay for a thing is to ask for it."

A wise man will extend this lesson to all parts of life, and know that it is always the part of prudence to face every claimant and pay every just demand on your time, your talents, or your heart. Always pay; for first or last you must pay your entire debt. Persons and events may stand for a time between you and justice, but it is only a postponement. You must pay at last your own debt. If you are wise you will dread a prosperity which only loads you with more. Benefit is the end of nature. But for every benefit which you receive, a tax is levied. He is great who confers the most benefits. He is base,—and that is the one base thing in the universe,—to receive favors and render none. In the order of nature we cannot render benefits to those from whom we receive them, or only seldom. But the benefit we receive must be rendered again, line for line, deed for deed, cent for cent, to somebody. Beware of too much good staying in your hand. It will fast corrupt and worm worms. Pay it away quickly in some sort.

Labor is watched over by the same pitiless laws. Cheapest, says the prudent, is the dearest labor. What we buy in a broom, a mat, a wagon, a knife, is some application of good sense to a common want. It is best to pay in your land a skilful gardener, or to buy good sense applied to gardening; in your sailor, good sense applied to navigation; in the house, good sense applied to cooking, sewing, serving; in your agent, good sense applied to accounts and affairs. So do you multiply your presence, or spread yourself throughout your estate. But because of the dual constitution of things, in labor as in life there can be no cheating. The thief steals from himself. The swindler swindles himself. For the real price of labor is knowledge and virtue, whereof wealth and credit are signs. These signs, like paper money, may be counterfeited or stolen, but that which they represent, namely, knowledge and virtue, cannot be counterfeited or stolen. These ends of labor cannot be answered but by real exertions of the mind, and in obedience to pure motives. The cheat, the defaulter, the gambler, cannot extort the benefit, cannot extort the knowledge of material and moral nature which his honest care and pains yield to the operative. The law of nature is, Do the thing, and you shall have the power; but they who do not the thing have not the power.

Human labor, through all its forms, from the sharpening of a stake to the construction of a city or an epic, is one immense illustration of the perfect compensation of the universe. Everywhere and always this law is sublime. The absolute balance of Give and Take, the doctrine that every thing has its price, and if that price is not paid, not that thing but something else is obtained, and that it is impossible to get anything without its price, is not less sublime in the columns of a ledger than in the budgets of states, in the laws of light and darkness, in all the action and reaction of nature. I cannot doubt that the high laws which each man sees ever implicated in those processes with which he is conversant, the stern ethics which sparkle on his chisel-edge, which are measured out by his plumb and foot-rule, which stand as manifest in the footing of the shop-bill as in the history of a state,—do recommend to him his trade, and though seldom named, exalt his business to his imagination.

The league between virtue and nature engages all things to assume a hostile front to vice. The beautiful laws and substances of the world persecute and whip the traitor. He finds that things are arranged for truth and benefit, but there is no den in the wide world to hide a rogue. Commit a crime, and the earth is made of glass. There is no such thing as concealment. Commit a crime, and it seems as if a coat of snow fell on the ground, such as reveals in the woods the track of every partridge and fox and squirrel and mole. You cannot recall the spoken word, you cannot wipe out the foot-track, you cannot draw up the ladder, so as to leave no inlet or clew. Always some damning circumstance transpires. The laws and substances of nature, water, snow, wind, gravitation, become penalties to the thief.

On the other hand the law holds with equal sureness for all right action. Love, and you shall be loved. All love is mathematically just, as much as the two sides of an algebraic equation. The good man has absolute good, which like fire turns every thing to its own nature, so that you cannot do him any harm; but as the royal armies sent against Napoleon, when he approached cast down their colors and from enemies became friends, so do disasters of all kinds, as sickness, offence, poverty, prove benefactors.

> Winds blow and waters roll
> Strength to the brave and power and deity,
> Yet in themselves are nothing.

The good are befriended even by weakness and defect. As no man had ever a point of pride that was not injurious to him, so no man had ever a defect that was not somewhere made useful to him. The stag in the fable admired his horns and blamed his feet, but when the hunter came, his feet saved him, and afterwards, caught in the thicket, his horns destroyed him. Every man in his lifetime needs to thank his faults. As no man thoroughly understands a truth until first he has contended against it, so no man has a thorough acquaintance with the hindrances or talents of men until he has suffered from the one and seen the triumph of the other over his own want of the same. Has he a defect of temper that unfits him to live in society? Thereby he is driven to entertain himself alone and acquire habits of self-help;

and thus, like the wounded oyster he mends his shell with pearl.

Our strength grows out of our weakness. Not until we are pricked and stung and sorely shot at, awakens the indignation which arms itself with secret forces. A great man is always willing to be little. Whilst he sits on the cushion of advantages, he goes to sleep. When he is pushed, tormented, defeated, he has a chance to learn something; he has been put on his wits, on his manhood; he has gained facts; learns his ignorance; is cured of the insanity of conceit; has got moderation and real skill. The wise man always throws himself on the side of his assailants. It is more his interest than it is theirs to find his weak point. The wound cicatrizes and falls off from him like a dead skin and when they would triumph, lo! he has passed on invulnerable. Blame is safer than praise. I hate to be defended in a newspaper. As long as all that is said is said against me, I feel a certain assurance of success. But as soon as honied words of praise are spoken for me I feel as one that lies unprotected before his enemies. In general, every evil to which we do not succumb is a benefactor. As the Sandwich Islander believes that the strength and valor of the enemy he kills passes into himself, so we gain the strength of the temptation we resist.

The same guards which protect us from disaster, defect and enmity, defend us, if we will, from selfishness and fraud. Bolts and bars are not the best of our institutions, nor is shrewdness in trade a mark of wisdom. Men suffer all their life long under the foolish superstition that they can be cheated. But it is as impossible for a man to be cheated by any one but himself, as for a thing to be and not to be at the same time. There is a third silent party to all our bargains. The nature and soul of things takes on itself the guaranty of the fulfilment of every contract, so that honest service cannot come to loss. If you serve an ungrateful master, serve him the more. Put God in your debt. Every stroke shall be repaid. The longer the payment is withholden, the better for you; for compound interest on compound interest is the rate and usage of this exchequer.

The history of persecution is a history of endeavors to cheat nature, to make water run up hill, to twist a rope of sand. It makes no difference whether the actors be many or one, a tyrant or a mob. A mob is a society of bodies voluntarily bereaving themselves of reason and traversing its work. The mob is man voluntarily descending to the nature of the beast. Its fit hour of activity is night. Its actions are insane, like its whole constitution. It persecutes a principle; it would whip a right; it would tar and feather justice, by inflicting fire and outrage upon the houses and persons of those who have these. It resembles the prank of boys, who run with fire-engines to put out the ruddy aurora streaming to the stars. The inviolate spirit turns their spite against the wrongdoers. The martyr cannot be dishonored. Every lash inflicted is a tongue of fame; every prison a more illustrious abode; every burned book or house enlightens the world; every suppressed or expunged word reverberates through the earth from side to side. The minds of men are at last aroused; reason looks out and justifies her own and malice finds all her work in vain. It is the whipper who is whipped and the tyrant who is undone.

Thus do all things preach the indifferency of circumstances. The man is all. Everything has two sides, a good and an evil. Every advantage has its tax. I learn to be content. But the doctrine of compensation is not the doctrine of indifferency. The thoughtless say, on hearing these representations,—What boots it to do well? there is one event to good and evil; if I gain any good I must pay for it; if I lose any good I gain some other; all actions are indifferent.

There is a deeper fact in the soul than compensation, to wit, its own nature. The soul is not a compensation, but a life. The soul *is*. Under all this running sea of circumstance, whose waters ebb and flow with perfect balance, lies the aboriginal abyss of real Being. Existence, or God, is not a relation or a part, but the whole. Being is the vast affirmative, excluding negation, self-balanced, and swallowing up all relations, parts and times within itself. Nature, truth, virtue, are the influx from thence. Vice is the absence or departure of the same. Nothing, Falsehood, may indeed stand as the great Night or shade on which as a back-ground the living universe paints itself forth; but no fact is begotten by it; it cannot work, for it is not. It cannot work any good; it cannot work any harm. It is harm inasmuch as it is worse not to be than to be.

We feel defrauded of the retribution due to evil acts, because the criminal adheres to his vice and contumacy and does not come to a crisis or judgment anywhere in visible nature. There is no stunning confutation of his nonsense before men and angels. Has he therefore outwitted the law? Inasmuch as he carries the malignity and the lie with him he so far decreases from nature. In some manner there will be a demonstration of the wrong to the understanding also; but, should we not see it, this deadly deduction makes square the eternal account.

Neither can it be said, on the other hand, that the gain of rectitude must be bought by any loss. There is no penalty to virtue; no penalty to wisdom; they are proper additions of being. In a virtuous action I properly *am;* in a virtuous act I add to the world; I plant into deserts conquered from Chaos and Nothing and see the darkness receding on the limits of the horizon. There can be no excess to love, none to knowledge, none to beauty, when these attributes are considered in the purest sense. The soul refuses all limits. It affirms in man always an Optimism, never a Pessimism.

His life is a progress, and not a station. His instinct is trust. Our instinct uses "more" and "less" in application to man, always of the *presence of the soul,* and not of its absence; the brave man is greater than the coward; the true, the benevolent, the wise, is more a man and not less, than the fool and knave. There is therefore no tax on the good of virtue, for that is the incoming of God himself, or absolute existence, without any comparative. All external good has its tax, and if it came without desert or sweat, has no root in me, and the next wind will blow it away. But all the good of nature is the soul's, and may be had if paid for in nature's lawful coin, that is, by labor which the heart and the head allow. I no longer wish to meet a good I do not earn, for example to find a pot of buried gold, knowing that it brings with it new responsibility. I do not wish more external goods, —neither possessions, nor honors, nor powers, nor persons. The gain is apparent; the tax is certain. But there is no tax on the knowledge that the compensation exists and that it is not desirable to dig up treasure. Herein I rejoice with a serene eternal peace. I contract the boundaries of possible mischief. I learn the wisdom of St. Bernard, "Nothing can work me damage except myself; the harm that I sustain I carry about with me, and never am a real sufferer but by my own fault."

In the nature of the soul is the compensation for the inequalities of condition. The radical tragedy of nature seems to be the distinction of More and Less. How can Less not feel the pain; how not feel indignation or malevolence towards More. Look at those who have less faculty, and one feels sad and knows not well what to make of it. Almost he shuns their eye; he fears they will upbraid God. What should they do? It seems a great injustice. But see the facts nearly and these mountainous inequalities vanish. Love reduces them as the sun melts the iceberg in the sea. The heart and soul of all men being one, this bitterness of *His* and *Mine* ceases. His is mine. I am my brother and my brother is me. If I feel overshadowed and outdone by great neighbors, I can get love; I can still receive; and he that loveth maketh his own the grandeur he loves. Thereby I make the discovery that my brother is my guardian, acting for me with the friendliest designs, and the estate I so admired and envied is my own. It is the eternal nature of the soul to appropriate and make all things its own. Jesus and Shakespeare are fragments of the soul, and by love I conquer and incorporate them in my own conscious domain. His virtue,—is not that mine? His wit,—if it cannot be made mine, it is not wit.

Such also is the natural history of calamity. The changes which break up at short intervals the prosperity of men are advertisements of a nature whose law is growth. Evermore it is the order of nature to grow, and every soul is by this intrinsic necessity quitting its whole system of things, its friends and home and laws and faith, as the shellfish crawls out of its beautiful but stony case, because it no longer admits of its growth, and slowly forms a new house. In proportion to the vigor of the individual these revolutions are frequent, until in some happier mind they are incessant and all worldly relations hang very loosely about him, becoming as it were a transparent fluid membrane through which the living form is always seen, and not, as in most men, an indurated heterogeneous fabric of many dates and of no settled character, in which the man is imprisoned. Then there can be enlargement, and the man of to-day scarcely recognizes the man of yesterday. And such should be the outward biography of man in time, a putting off of dead circumstances day by day, as he renews his raiment day by day. But to us, in our lapsed estate, resting, not advancing, resisting, not coöperating with the divine expansion, this growth comes by shocks.

We cannot part with our friends. We cannot let our angels go. We do not see that they only go out that archangels may come in. We are idolaters of the old. We do not believe in the riches of the soul, in its proper eternity and omnipresence. We do not believe there is any force in to-day to rival or re-create that beautiful yesterday. We linger in the ruins of the old tent where once we had bread and shelter and organs, nor believe that the spirit can feed, cover and nerve us again. We cannot again find aught so dear, so sweet, so graceful. But we sit and weep in vain. The voice of the Almighty saith, "Up and onward forevermore!" We cannot stay amid the ruins. Neither will we rely on the New; and so we walk ever with reverted eyes, like those monsters who look backwards.

And yet the compensations of calamity are made apparent to the understanding also, after long intervals of time. A fever, a mutilation, a cruel disappointment, a loss of wealth, a loss of friends, seems at the moment unpaid loss, and unpayable. But the sure years reveal the deep remedial force that underlies all facts. The death of a dear friend, wife, brother, lover, which seemed nothing but privation, somewhat later assumes the aspect of a guide or genius; for it commonly operates revolutions in our way of life, terminates an epoch of infancy or of youth which was waiting to be closed, breaks up a wonted occupation, or a household, or style of living, and allows the formation of new ones more friendly to the growth of character. It permits or constrains the formation of new acquaintances and the reception of new influences that prove of the first importance to the next years; and the man or woman who would have remained a sunny garden-flower, with no room for its roots and too much sunshine for its head, by the falling of the walls and the neglect of the gardener is made the banian of the forest, yielding shade and fruit to wide neighborhoods of men.

# NATURE

The rounded world is fair to see,
Nine times folded in mystery:
Though baffled seers cannot impart
The secret of its laboring heart,
Throb thine with Nature's throbbing breast,
And all is clear from east to west.
Spirit that lurks each form within
Beckons to spirit of its kin;
Self-kindled every atom glows,
And hints the future which it owes.

THERE are days which occur in this climate, at almost any season of the year, wherein the world reaches its perfection, when the air, the heavenly bodies, and the earth, make a harmony, as if nature would indulge her offspring; when, in these bleak upper sides of the planet, nothing is to desire that we have heard of the happiest latitudes, and we bask in the shining hours of Florida and Cuba; when everything that has life gives sign of satisfaction, and the cattle that lie on the ground seem to have great and tranquil thoughts. These halcyons may be looked for with a little more assurance in that pure October weather, which we distinguish by the name of the Indian Summer. The day, immeasurably long, sleeps over the broad hills and warm wide fields. To have lived through all its sunny hours, seems longevity enough. The solitary places do not seem quite lonely. At the gates of the forest, the surprised man of the world is forced to leave his city estimates of great and small, wise and foolish. The knapsack of custom falls off his back with the first step he makes into these precincts. Here is sanctity which shames our religions, and reality which discredits our heroes. Here we find nature to be the circumstance which dwarfs every other circumstance, and judges like a god all men that come to her. We have crept out of our close and crowded houses into the night and morning, and we see what majestic beauties daily wrap us in their bosom. How willingly we would escape the barriers which render them comparatively impotent, escape the sophistication and second thought, and suffer nature to entrance us. The tempered light of the woods is like a perpetual morning, and is stimulating and heroic. The anciently reported spells of these places creep on us. The stems of pines, hemlocks, and oaks, almost gleam like iron on the excited eye. The incommunicable trees begin to persuade us to live with them, and quit our life of solemn trifles. Here no history, or church, or state, is interpolated on the divine sky and the immortal year. How easily we might walk onward into the opening landscape, absorbed by new pictures, and by thoughts fast succeeding each other, until by degrees the recollection of home was crowded out of the mind, all memory obliterated by the tyranny of the present, and we were led in triumph by nature.

These enchantments are medicinal, they sober and heal us. These are plain pleasures, kindly and native to us. We come to our own, and make friends with matter, which the ambitious chatter of the schools would persuade us to despise. We never can part with it; the mind loves its old home: as water to our thirst, so is the rock, the ground, to our eyes, and hands, and feet. It is firm water: it is cold flame: what health, what affinity! Ever an old friend, ever like a dear friend and brother, when we chat affectedly with strangers, comes in this honest face, and takes a grave liberty with us, and shames us out of our nonsense. Cities give not the human senses room enough. We go out daily and nightly to feed the eyes on the horizon, and require so much scope, just as we need water for our bath. There are all degrees of natural influence, from these quarantine powers of nature, up to her dearest and gravest ministrations to the imagination and the soul. There is the bucket of cold water from the spring, the wood-fire to which the chilled traveller rushes for safety,—and there is the sublime moral of autumn and of noon. We nestle in nature, and draw our living as parasites from her roots and grains, and we receive glances from the heavenly bodies, which call us to solitude, and foretell the remotest future. The blue zenith is the point in which romance and reality meet. I think, if we should be rapt away into all that we dream of heaven, and should converse with Gabriel and Uriel, the upper sky would be all that would remain of our furniture.

It seems as if the day was not wholly profane, in which we have given heed to some natural object. The fall of snowflakes in a still air, preserving to each crystal its perfect form; the blowing of sleet over a wide sheet of water, and over plains; the waving rye-field; the mimic waving of acres of houstonia, whose innumerable florets whiten and ripple before the eye; the reflections of trees and flowers in glassy lakes; the musical steaming odorous south wind, which converts all trees to windharps; the crackling and spurting of hemlock in the flames, or of pine logs, which yield glory to the walls and faces in the sitting-room,—these are the music and pictures of the most ancient religion. My house stands in low land, with limited outlook, and on the skirt of the village.

But I go with my friend to the shore of our little river, and with one stroke of the paddle, I leave the village politics and personalities, yes, and the world of villages and personalities behind, and pass into a delicate realm of sunset and moonlight, too bright almost for spotted man to enter without noviciate and probation. We penetrate bodily this incredible beauty: we dip our hands in this painted element: our eyes are bathed in these lights and forms. A holiday, a villeggiatura, a royal revel, the proudest, most heart-rejoicing festival that valor and beauty, power and taste, ever decked and enjoyed, establishes itself on the instant. These sunset clouds, these delicately emerging stars, with their private and ineffable glances, signify it and proffer it. I am taught the poorness of our invention, the ugliness of towns and palaces. Art and luxury have early learned that they must work as enchantment and sequel to this original beauty. I am over-instructed for my return. Henceforth I shall be hard to please. I cannot go back to toys. I am grown expensive and sophisticated. I can no longer live without elegance: but a countryman shall be my master of revels. He who knows the most, he who knows what sweets and virtues are in the ground, the waters, the plants, the heavens, and how to come at these enchantments, is the rich and royal man. Only as far as the masters of the world have called in nature to their aid, can they reach the height of magnificence. This is the meaning of their hanging-gardens, villas, garden-houses, islands, parks, and preserves, to back their faulty personality with these strong accessories. I do not wonder that the landed interest should be invincible in the state with these dangerous auxiliaries. These bribe and invite; not kings, not palaces, not men, not women, but these tender and poetic stars, eloquent of secret promises. We heard what the rich man said, we knew of his villa, his grove, his wine, and his company, but the provocation and point of the invitation came out of these beguiling stars. In their soft glances, I see what men strove to realize in some Versailles, or Paphos, or Ctesiphon. Indeed, it is the magical lights of the horizon, and the blue sky for the background, which save all our works of art, which were otherwise bawbles. When the rich tax the poor with servility and obsequiousness, they should consider the effect of men reputed to be the possesors of nature, on imaginative minds. Ah! if the rich were rich as the poor fancy riches! A boy hears a military band play on the field at night, and he has kings and queens and famous chivalry palpably before him. He hears the echoes of a horn in a hill country, in the Notch Mountains, for example, which converts the mountains into an Æolian harp, and this supernatural *tiralira* restores to him the Dorian mythology, Apollo, Diana, and all divine hunters and huntresses. Can a musical note be so lofty, so haughtily beautiful! To the poor young poet, thus fabulous is his picture of society; he is loyal; he respects the rich; they are rich for the sake of his imagination; how poor his fancy would be, if they were not rich! That they have some high-fenced grove, which they call a park; that they live in larger and better-garnished saloons than he has visited, and go in coaches, keeping only the society of the elegant, to watering-places, and to distant cities, are the groundwork from which he has delineated estates of romance, compared with which their actual possessions are shanties and paddocks. The muse herself betrays her son, and enhances the gifts of wealth and well-born beauty, by a radiation out of the air, and clouds, and forests that skirt the road,—a certain haughty favor, as if from patrician genii to patricians, a kind of aristocracy in nature, a prince of the power of the air.

The moral sensibility which makes Edens and Tempes so easily, may not be always found, but the material landscape is never far off. We can find these enchantments without visiting the Como Lake, or the Madeira Islands. We exaggerate the praises of local scenery. In every landscape, the point of astonishment is the meeting of the sky and the earth, and that is seen from the first hillock as well as from the top of the Alleghanies. The stars at night stoop down over the brownest, homeliest common, with all the spiritual magnificence which they shed on the Campagna, or on the marble deserts of Egypt. The uprolled clouds and the colors of morning and evening, will transfigure maples and alders. The difference between landscape and landscape is small, but there is great difference in the beholders. There is nothing so wonderful in any particular landscape, as the necessity of being beautiful under which every landscape lies. Nature cannot be surprised in undress. Beauty breaks in everywhere.

But it is very easy to outrun the sympathy of readers on this topic, which schoolmen called *natura naturata,* or nature passive. One can hardly speak directly of it without excess. It is as easy to broach in mixed companies what is called "the subject of religion." A susceptible person does not like to indulge his tastes in this kind, without the apology of some trivial necessity; he goes to see a wood-lot, or to look at the crops, or to fetch a plant or a mineral from a remote locality, or he carries a fowling-piece, or a fishing-rod. I suppose this shame must have a good reason. A dilettantism in nature is barren and unworthy. The fop of fields is no better than his brother of Broadway. Men are naturally hunters and inquisitive of wood-craft, and I suppose that such a gazetteer as wood-cutters and Indians should furnish facts for, would take place in the most sumptuous drawing-rooms of all the "Wreaths" and "Flora's chaplets" of the book-shops; yet ordinarily, whether we are too clumsy for so subtle a topic, or from whatever cause, as soon as men begin to write on nature, they fall into euphuism. Frivolity is a most unfit tribute to Pan, who ought to be represented in the mythology as the most continent of gods. I would not be frivolous before the admirable reserve and prudence of time, yet I cannot renounce the right of returning often to this old topic. The multitude of false churches accredits the true religion. Literature, poetry, science, are the homage of man to this unfathomed secret, concerning which no sane man can affect an indifference or incuriosity. Nature is loved by what is best in us. It is loved as the city of God, although, or rather because there is no citizen. The sunset is unlike anything that is underneath it: it wants men. And the beauty of nature must always seem unreal and mocking, until the landscape has human figures, that are as good as itself. If there were good men, there would never be this rapture in nature. If the king is in the palace, nobody looks at the walls. It is when he is gone, and the house is filled with grooms and gazers, that we turn from the people, to find relief in the majestic men that are suggested by the pictures and the architecture. The critics who complain of the sickly separation of the beauty of nature from the thing to be done, must consider that our hunting of the picturesque is inseparable from our protest against false society. Man is fallen; nature is erect, and serves as a differential thermometer, detecting the presence or absence of the divine sentiment in man. By fault of our dulness and selfishness, we are looking up to nature, but when we are convalescent, nature will look up to us. We see the foaming brook with compunction: if our own life flowed with the right energy, we should shame the brook. The stream of zeal sparkles with real fire, and not with reflex rays of sun and moon. Nature may be as selfishly studied as trade. Astronomy to the selfish becomes astrology; Psychology, mesmerism (with intent to show where our spoons are gone); and anatomy and physiology, become phrenology and palmistry.

But taking timely warning, and leaving many things unsaid on this topic, let us not longer omit our homage to the Efficient Nature, *natura naturans,* the quick cause, before which all forms flee as the driven snow; itself secret, its works driven before it in flocks and multitudes, (as the ancient represented nature by Proteus, a shepherd,) and in undescribable variety. It publishes itself in creatures, reaching from particles and spicula, through transformation on transformation to the highest symmetries, arriving at consummate results without a shock or a leap. A little heat, that is, a little motion, is all that differences the bald, dazzling white, and deadly cold poles of the earth from the prolific tropical climates. All changes pass without violence, by reason of the two cardinal conditions of boundless space and boundless time. Geology has initiated us into the secularity of nature, and taught us to disuse our dame-school measures, and exchange our Mosiac and Ptolemaic schemes for her large style. We knew nothing rightly, for want of perspective. Now we learn what patient periods must round themselves before the rock is formed, then before the rock is broken, and the first lichen race has disintegrated the thinnest external plate into soil, and opened the door for the remote Flora, Fauna, Ceres, and Pomona, to come in. How far off yet is the trilobite! how far the quadruped! how inconceivably remote is man! All duly arrive, and then race after race of men. It is a long way from granite to the oyster; farther yet to Plato, and the preaching of the immortality of the soul. Yet all must come, as surely as the first atom has two sides.

Motion or change, and identity or rest, are the first and second secrets of nature: Motion and Rest. The whole code of her laws may be written on the thumbnail, or the signet of a ring. The whirling bubble on the surface of a brook, admits us to the secret of the mechanics of the sky. Every shell on the beach is a key to it. A little water made to rotate in a cup explains the formation of the simpler shells; the addition of matter from year to year, arrives at last at the most complex form; and yet so poor is nature with all her craft, that from the beginning to the end of the universe, she has but one stuff,—but one stuff with its two ends, to serve up all her dream-like variety. Compound it how she will, star, sand, fire, water, tree, man, it is still one stuff, and betrays the same properties.

Nature is always consistent, though she feigns to contravene her own laws. She keeps her laws, and seems to transcend them. She arms and equips an animal to find its place and living in the earth, and, at the same time, she arms and equips another animal to destroy it. Space exists to divide creatures; but by clothing the sides of a bird with a few feathers, she gives him a petty omnipresence. The direction is forever onward, but the artist still goes back for materials, and begins again with the first elements on the most advanced stage: otherwise, all goes to ruin. If we look at her work, we seem to catch a glance of a system in transition. Plants are the young of the world, vessels of health and vigor; but they grope ever upward toward consciousness; the trees are imperfect men, and seem to bemoan their imprisonment, rooted in the ground. The animal is the novice and probationer of a more advanced order. The men, though young, having tasted the first drop from the cup of thought, are already dissipated: the maples and ferns are still uncorrupt; yet no doubt, when they come to consciousness, they too will curse and swear. Flowers so strictly belong to youth, that we adult men soon come to feel that their beautiful generations concern not us: we have had our day; now let the children have theirs. The flowers jilt us, and we are old bachelors with our ridiculous tenderness.

Things are so strictly related, that according to the skill of the eye, from any one object the parts and properties of any other may be predicted. If we had eyes to see it, a bit of stone from the city wall would certify us of the necessity that man must exist, as readily as the city. That identity makes us all one, and reduces to nothing great intervals on our customary scale. We talk of deviations from natural life, as if artificial life were not also natural. The smoothest curled courtier in the boudoirs of a palace has an animal nature, rude and aboriginal as a white bear, omnipotent to its own ends, and is directly related, there amid essences and billets-doux, to Himmaleh mountain-chains, and the axis of the globe. If we consider how much we are nature's, we need not be superstitious about towns, as if that terrific or benefic force did not find us there also, and fashion cities. Nature who made the mason, made the house. We may easily hear too much of rural influences. The cool disengaged air of natural objects, makes them enviable to us, chafed and irritable creatures with red faces, and we think we shall be as grand as they, if we camp out and eat roots; but let us be men instead of woodchucks, and the oak and the elm shall gladly serve us, though we sit in chairs of ivory on carpets of silk.

This guiding identity runs through all the surprises and contrasts of the piece, and characterizes every law. Man carries the world in his head, the whole astronomy and chemistry suspended in a thought. Because the history of nature is charactered in his brain, therefore is he the prophet and discoverer of her secrets. Every known fact in natural science was divined by the presentiment of somebody, before it was actually verified. A man does not tie his shoe without recognizing laws which bind the farthest regions of nature: moon, plant, gas, crystal, are concrete geometry and numbers. Common sense knows its own, and recognizes the fact at first sight in chemical experiment. The common sense of Franklin, Dalton, Davy, and Black, is the same common sense which made the arrangements which now it discovers.

If the identity expresses organized rest, the counter action runs also into organization. The astronomers said, 'Give us matter, and a little motion, and we will construct the universe. It is not enough that we should have matter, we must also have a single impulse, one shove to launch the mass, and generate the harmony of the centrifugal and centripetal forces. Once heave the ball from the hand, and we can show how all this mighty order grew.'—'A very unreasonable postulate,' said the metaphysicians, 'and a plain begging of the question. Could you not prevail to know the genesis of projection, as well as the continuation of it?' Nature, meanwhile, had not waited for the discussion, but, right or wrong, bestowed the impulse, and the balls rolled. It was no great affair, a mere push, but the astronomers were right in making much of it, for there is no end to the consequences of the act. That famous aboriginal push propagates itself through all the balls of the system, and through every atom of every ball, through all the races of creatures, and through the history and performances of every individual. Exaggeration is in the course of things. Nature sends no creature, no man into the world, without adding a small excess of his proper quality. Given the planet, it is still necessary to add the impulse; so, to every creature nature added a little violence of direction in its proper path, a shove to put it on its way; in every instance, a slight generosity, a drop too much. Without electricity the air would rot, and without this violence of direction, which men and women have, without a spice of bigot and fanatic, no excitement, no efficiency. We aim above the mark, to hit the mark. Every act hath some falsehood of exaggeration in it. And when now and then comes along some sad, sharp-eyed man, who sees how paltry a game is played, and refuses to play, but blabs the secret;—how then? is the bird flown? O no, the wary Nature sends a new troop of fairer forms, of lordlier youths, with a little more excess of direction to hold them fast to their several aim; makes them a little wrong-headed in that direction in which they are rightest, and on goes the game again with new whirl, for a generation or two more. The child with his sweet pranks, the fool of his senses, commanded by every sight and sound, without any power to compare and rank his sensations, abandoned to a whistle or a painted chip, to a lead dragoon, or a gingerbread-dog, individualizing everything, generalizing nothing, delighted with every new thing, lies down at night overpowered by the fatigue, which this day of continual pretty madness has incurred. But Nature has answered her purpose with the curly, dimpled lunatic. She has tasked every faculty, and has secured the symmetrical growth of the bodily frame, by all these attitudes and exertions,—an end of the first importance, which could not be trusted to any care less perfect than her own. This glitter, this opaline lustre plays round the top of every toy to his eye, to ensure his fidelity, and he is deceived to his good. We are made alive and kept alive by the same arts. Let the stoics say what they please, we do not eat for the good of living, but because the meat is savory and the appetite is keen. The vegetable life does not content itself with casting from the flower or the tree a single seed, but it fills the air and earth with a prodigality of seeds, that, if thousands perish, thousands may plant themselves, that hundreds may come up, that tens may live to maturity, that, at least, one may replace the parent. All things betray the same calculated profusion. The excess of fear with which the animal frame is hedged round, shrinking from cold, starting at sight of a snake, or at a sudden noise, protects us, through a multitude of groundless alarms, from some one real danger at last. The lover seeks in marriage his private felicity and perfection, with no prospective end; and nature hides in his happiness her own end, namely, progeny, or the perpetuity of the race.

But the craft with which the world is made, runs also into the mind and character of men. No man is quite sane; each has a vein of folly in his composition, a slight determination of blood to the head, to make sure of holding him hard to some one point which nature had taken to heart. Great causes are never tried on their merits; but the cause is reduced to particulars to suit the size of the partisans, and the contention is ever hottest on minor matters. Not less remarkable is the overfaith of each man in the importance of what he has to do or say. The poet, the prophet, has a higher value for what he utters than any hearer, and therefore it gets spoken. The strong, self-complacent Luther declares with an emphasis, not to be mistaken, that "God himself cannot do without wise men." Jacob Behmen and George Fox betray their egotism in the pertinacity of their controversial tracts, and James Naylor once suffered himself to be worshipped as the Christ. Each prophet comes presently to identify himself with his thought, and to esteem his hat and shoes sacred. However this may discredit such persons with the judicious, it helps them with the people, as it gives heat, pungency, and publicity to their words. A similar experience is not infrequent in private life. Each young and ardent person writes a diary, in which, when the hours of prayer and penitence arrive, he inscribes his soul. The pages thus written are, to him, burning and fragrant: he reads them on his knees by midnight and by the morning star; he wets them with his tears: they are sacred; too good for the world, and hardly yet to be shown to the dearest friend. This is the man-child that is born to the soul, and her life still circulates in the babe. The umbilical cord has not yet been cut. After some time has elapsed, he begins to wish to admit his friend to this hallowed experience, and with hesitation, yet with firmness, exposes the pages to his eye. Will they not burn his eyes? The friend coldly turns them over, and passes from the writing to conversation, with easy transition, which strikes the other party with astonishment and vexation. He cannot suspect the writing itself. Days and nights of fervid life, of communion with angels of darkness and of light, have engraved their shadowy characters on that tearstained book. He suspects the intelligence or the heart of his friend. Is there then no friend? He cannot yet credit that one may have impressive experience, and yet may not know how to put his private fact into literature; and perhaps the discovery that wisdom has other tongues and ministers than we, that though we should hold our peace, the truth would not the less be spoken, might check injuriously the flames of our zeal. A man can only speak, so long as he does not feel his speech to be partial and inadequate. It is partial, but he does not see it to be so, whilst he utters it. As soon as he is released from the instinctive and particular, and sees its partiality, he shuts his mouth in disgust. For, no man can write anything, who does not think that what he writes is for the time the history of the world; or do anything well, who does not esteem his work to be of importance. My work may be of none, but I must not think it of none, or I shall not do it with impunity.

In like manner, there is throughout nature something mocking, something that leads us on and on, but arrives nowhere, keeps no faith with us. All promise outruns the performance. We live in a system of approximations. Every end is prospective of some other end, which is also temporary; a round and final success nowhere. We are encamped in nature, not domesticated. Hunger and thirst lead us on to eat and to drink; but bread and wine, mix and cook them how you will, leave us hungry and thirsty, after the stomach is full. It is the same with all our arts and performances. Our music, our poetry, our language itself are not satisfactions, but suggestions. The hunger for wealth, which reduces the planet to a garden, fools the eager pursuer. What is the end sought? Plainly to secure the ends of good sense and beauty from the intrusion of deformity or vulgarity of any kind. But what an operose method! What a train of means to secure a little conversation! This palace of brick and stone, these servants, this kitchen, these stables, horses and equipage, this bankstock, and file of mortgages; trade to all the world, country-house and cottage by the waterside, all for a little conversation, high, clear, and spiritual! Could it not be had as well by beggars on the highway? No, all these things came from successive efforts of these beggars to remove friction from the wheels of life, and give opportunity. Conversation, character, were the avowed ends; wealth was good as it appeased the animal cravings, cured the smoky chimney, silenced the creaking door, brought friends together in a warm and quiet room, and kept the children and the dinner-table in a different apartment. Thought, virtue, beauty, were the ends; but it was known that men of thought and virtue sometimes had the headache, or wet feet, or could lose good time whilst the room was getting warm in winter days. Unluckily, in the exertions necessary to remove these inconveniences, the main attention has been diverted to this object; the old aims have been lost sight of, and to remove friction has come to be the end. That is the ridicule of rich men; and Boston, London, Vienna, and now the governments generally of the world, are cities and governments of the rich, and the masses are not men, but *poor men,* that is, men who would be rich; this is the ridicule of the class, that they arrive with pains and sweat and fury nowhere; when all is done, it is for nothing. They are like one who has interrupted the conversation of a company to make his speech, and now has forgotten what he went to say. The appearance strikes the eye everywhere of an aimless society, of aimless nations. Were the ends of nature so great and cogent as to exact this immense sacrifice of men?

Quite analogous to the deceits in life, there is, as might be expected, a similar effect on the eye from the face of external nature. There is in woods and waters a certain enticement and flattery, together with a failure to yield a present satisfaction. This disappointment is felt in every landscape. I have seen the softness and beauty of the summer-clouds floating feathery overhead, enjoying, as it seemed, their height and privilege of motion, whilst yet they appeared not so much the drapery of this place and hour, as fore-looking to some pavilions and gardens of festivity beyond. It is an odd jealousy: but the poet finds himself not near enough to his object. The pine-tree, the river, the bank of flowers before him, does not seem to be nature. Nature is still elsewhere. This or this is but outskirt and far-off reflection and echo of the triumph that has passed by, and is now at its glancing splendor and heyday, perchance in the neighboring fields, or, if you stand in the field, then in the adjacent woods. The present object shall give you this sense of stillness that follows a pageant which has just gone by. What splendid distance, what recesses of ineffable pomp and loveliness in the sunset! But who can go where they are, or lay his hand or plant his foot thereon? Off they fall from the round world forever and ever. It is the same among the men and women, as among the silent trees, always a referred existence, an absence, never a presence and satisfaction. It is that beauty can never be grasped? in persons and in landscape is equally inaccessible? The accepted and betrothed lover has lost the wildest charm of his maiden in her acceptance of him. She was heaven whilst he pursued her as a star: she cannot be heaven, if she stoops to such a one as he.

What shall we say of this omnipresent appearance of that first projectile impulse, of this flattery and balking of so many well-meaning creatures? Must we not suppose somewhere in the universe a slight treachery and derision? Are we not engaged to a serious resentment of this use that is made of us? Are we tickled trout, and fools of nature? One look at the face of heaven and earth lays all petulance at rest, and soothes us to wiser convictions. To the intelligent, nature converts itself into a vast promise, and will not be rashly explained. Her secret is untold. Many and many an Œdipus arrives: he has the whole mystery teeming in his brain. Alas! the same sorcery has spoiled his skill; no syllable can he shape on his lips. Her mighty orbit vaults like the fresh rainbow into the deep, but no archangel's wing was yet strong enough to follow it, and report of the return of the curve. But it also appears, that our actions are seconded and disposed to greater conclusions than we designed. We are escorted on every hand through life by spiritual agents, and a beneficent purpose lies in wait for us. We cannot bandy words with nature, or deal with her as we deal with persons. If we measure our individual forces against hers, we may easily feel as if we were the sport of an insuperable destiny. But if, instead of identifying ourselves with the work, we feel that the soul of the workman streams through us, we shall find the peace of the morning dwelling first in our hearts, and the fathomless powers of gravity and chemistry, and, over them, of life, preëxisting within us in their highest form.

The uneasiness which the thought of our helplessness in the chain of causes occasions us, results from looking too much at one condition of nature, namely, Motion. But the drag is never taken from the wheel. Wherever the impulse exceeds, the Rest or Identity insinuates its compensation. All over the wide fields of earth grows the prunella or self-heal. After every foolish day we sleep off the fumes and furies of its hours; and though we are always engaged with particulars, and often enslaved to them, we bring with us to every experiment the innate universal laws. These, while they exist in the mind as ideas, stand around us in nature forever embodied, a present sanity to expose and cure the insanity of men. Our servitude to particulars betrays into a hundred foolish expectations. We anticipate a new era from the invention of a locomotive, or a balloon; the new engine brings with it the old checks. They say that by electro-magnetism, your salad shall be grown from the seed, whilst your fowl is roasting for dinner: it is a symbol of our modern aims and endeavors,—of our condensation and acceleration of objects: but nothing is gained: nature cannot be cheated: man's life is but seventy salads long, grow they swift or grow they slow. In these checks and impossibilities, however, we find our advantage, not less than in the impulses. Let the victory fall where it will, we are on that side. And the knowledge that we traverse the whole scale of being, from the centre to the poles of nature, and have some stake in every possibility, lends that sublime lustre to death, which philosophy and religion have too outwardly and literally striven to express in the popular doctrine of the immortality of the soul. The reality is more excellent than the report. Here is no ruin, no discontinuity, no spent ball. The divine circulations never rest nor linger. Nature is the incarnation of a thought, and turns to a thought, again, as ice becomes water and gas. The world is mind precipitated, and the volatile essence is forever escaping again into the state of free thought. Hence the virtue and pungency of the influence on the mind of natural objects, whether inorganic or organized. Man imprisoned, man crystallized, man vegetative, speaks to man impersonated. That power which does not respect quantity, which makes the whole and the particle its equal channel, delegates its smile to the morning, and distils its essence into every drop of rain. Every moment instructs, and every object: for wisdom is infused into every form. It has been poured into us as blood; it convulsed us as pain; it slid into us as pleasure; it enveloped us in dull, melancholy days, or in days of cheerful labor; we did not guess its essence, until after a long time.

# FRIENDSHIP

A ruddy drop of manly blood
The surging sea outweighs;
The world uncertain comes and goes,
The lover rooted stays.
I fancied he was fled,
And, after many a year,
Glowed unexhausted kindliness
Like daily sunrise there.
My careful heart was free again,—
O friend, my bosom said,
Through thee alone the sky is arched,
Through thee the rose is red,
All things through thee take nobler form
And look beyond the earth,
The mill-round of our fate appears
A sun-path in thy worth.
Me too thy nobleness has taught
To master my despair;
The fountains of my hidden life
Are through thy friendship fair.

We have a great deal more kindness than is ever spoken. Maugre all the selfishness that chills like east winds the world, the whole human family is bathed with an element of love like a fine ether. How many persons we meet in houses, whom we scarcely speak to, whom yet we honor, and who honor us! How many we see in the street, or sit with in church, whom, though silently, we warmly rejoice to be with! Read the language of these wandering eye-beams. The heart knoweth.

The effect of the indulgence of this human affection is a certain cordial exhilaration. In poetry and in common speech the emotions of benevolence and complacency which are felt towards others are likened to the material effects of fire; so swift, or much more swift, more active, more cheering, are these fine inward irradiations. From the highest degree of passionate love to the lowest degree of good-will, they make the sweetness of life.

Our intellectual and active powers increase with our affection. The scholar sits down to write, and all his years of meditation do not furnish him with one good thought or happy expression; but it is necessary to write a letter to a friend,—and forthwith troops of gentle thoughts invest themselves, on every hand, with chosen words. See, in any house where virtue and self-respect abide, the palpitation which the approach of a stranger causes. A commended stranger is expected and announced, and an uneasiness betwixt pleasure and pain invades all the hearts of a household. His arrival almost brings fear to the good hearts that would welcome him. The house is dusted, all things fly into their places, the old coat is exchanged for the new, and they must get up a dinner if they can. Of a commended stranger, only the good report is told by others, only the good and new is heard by us. He stands to us for humanity. He is what we wish. Having imagined and invested him, we ask how we should stand related in conversation and action with such a man, and are uneasy with fear. The same idea exalts conversation with him. We talk better than we are wont. We have the nimblest fancy, a richer memory, and our dumb devil has taken leave for the time. For long hours we can continue a series of sincere, graceful, rich communications, drawn from the oldest, secretest experience, so that they who sit by, of our own kinsfolk and acquaintance, shall feel a lively surprise at our unusual powers. But as soon as the stranger begins to intrude his partialities, his definitions, his defects into the conversation, it is all over. He has heard the first, the last and best he will ever hear from us. He is no stranger now. Vulgarity, ignorance, misapprehension are old acquaintances. Now, when he comes, he may get the order, the dress and the dinner,—but the throbbing of the heart and the communications of the soul, no more.

Pleasant are these jets of affection which relume a young world for me again. Delicious is a just and firm encounter of two, in a thought, in a feeling. How beautiful, on their approach to this beating heart, the steps and forms of the gifted and the true! The moment we indulge our affections, the earth is metamorphosed; there is no winter and no night; all tragedies, all ennuis vanish,—all duties even; nothing fills the proceeding eternity but the forms all radiant of beloved persons. Let the soul be assured that somewhere in the universe it should rejoin its friend, and it would be content and cheerful alone for a thousand years.

I awoke this morning with devout thanksgiving for my friends, the old and the new. Shall I not call God the Beautiful, who daily showeth himself so to me in his gifts? I chide society, I embrace solitude, and yet I am not so ungrateful as not to see the wise, the lovely and the noble-minded, as from time to time they pass my gate. Who hears me, who understands me, becomes mine,—a possession for all time. Nor is Nature so poor but she gives me this joy several times, and thus we weave social threads of our own, a new web of relations; and, as many thoughts in succession substantiate themselves, we shall by and by stand in a new world of our own creation, and no longer strangers and pilgrims in a traditionary globe. My friends have come to me unsought. The great God gave them to me. By oldest right, by the divine affinity of virtue with itself, I find them, or rather not I, but the Deity in me and in them derides and cancels the thick walls of individual character, relation, age, sex, circumstance, at which he usually connives, and now makes many one. High thanks I owe you, excellent lovers, who carry out the world for me to new and noble depths, and enlarge the meaning of all my thoughts. These are new poetry of the first Bard,—poetry without stop,—hymn, ode and epic, poetry still flowing, Apollo and the Muses chanting still. Will these too separate themselves from me again, or some of them? I know not, but I fear it not; for my relation to them is so pure that we hold by simple affinity, and the Genius of my life being thus social, the same affinity will exert its energy on whomsoever is as noble as these men and women, wherever I may be.

I confess to an extreme tenderness of nature on this point. It is almost dangerous to me to "crush the sweet poison of misused wine" of the affections. A new person is to me a great event and hinders me from sleep. I have often had fine fancies about persons which have given me delicious hours; but the joy ends in the day; it yields no fruit. Thought is not born of it; my action is very little modified. I must feel pride in my friend's accomplishments as if they were mine, and a property in his virtues. I feel as warmly when he is praised, as the lover when he hears applause of his engaged maiden. We over-estimate the conscience of our friend. His goodness seems better than our goodness, his nature finer, his temptations less. Everything that is his,—his name, his form, his dress, books and instruments,—fancy enhances. Our own thought sounds new and larger from his mouth.

Yet the systole and diastole of the heart are not without their analogy in the ebb and flow of love. Friendship, like the immortality of the soul, is too good to be believed. The lover, beholding his maiden, half knows that she is not verily that which he worships; and in the golden hour of friendship we are surprised with shades of suspicion and unbelief. We doubt that we bestow on our hero the virtues in which he shines, and afterwards worship the form to which we have ascribed this divine inhabitation. In strictness, the soul does not respect men as it respects itself. In strict science all persons underlie the same condition of an infinite remoteness. Shall we fear to cool our love by mining for the metaphysical foundation of this Elysian temple? Shall I not be as real as the things I see? If I am, I shall not fear to know them for what they are. Their essence is not less beautiful than their appearance, though it needs finer organs for its apprehension. The root of the plant is not unsightly to science, though for chaplets and festoons we cut the stem short. And I must hazard the production of the bald fact amidst these pleasing reveries, though it should prove an Egyptian skull at our banquet. A man who stands united with his thought conceives magnificently of himself. He is conscious of a universal success, even though bought by uniform particular failures. No advantages, no powers, no gold or force, can be any match for him. I cannot choose but rely on my own poverty more than on your wealth. I cannot make your consciousness tantamount to mine. Only the star dazzles; the planet has a faint, moonlike ray. I hear what you say of the admirable parts and tried temper of the party you praise, but I see well that, for all his purple cloaks, I shall not like him, unless he is at least a poor Greek like me. I cannot deny it, O friend, that the vast shadow of the Phenomenal includes thee also in its pied and painted immensity,—thee also, compared with whom all else is shadow. Thou art not Being, as Truth is, as Justice is,—thou art not my soul, but a picture and effigy of that. Thou hast come to me lately, and already thou art seizing thy hat and cloak. Is it not that the soul puts forth friends as the tree puts forth leaves, and presently, by the germination of new buds, extrudes the old leaf? The law of nature is alternation for evermore. Each electrical state superinduces the opposite. The soul environs itself with friends that it may enter into a grander self-acquaintance or solitude; and it goes alone for a season that it may exalt its conversation or society. This method betrays itself along the whole history of our personal relations. The instinct of affection revives the hope of union with our mates, and the returning sense of insulation recalls us from the chase. Thus every man passes his life in the search after friendship, and if he should record his true sentiment, he might write a letter like this to each new candidate for his love:—

DEAR FRIEND,

If I was sure of thee, sure of thy capacity, sure to match my mood with thine, I should never think again of trifles in relation to thy comings and goings. I am not very wise; my moods are quite attainable, and I respect thy genius; it is to me as yet unfathomed; yet dare I not presume in thee a perfect intelligence of me, and so thou art to me a delicious torment. Thine ever, or never.

Yet these uneasy pleasures and fine pains are for curiosity and not for life. They are not to be indulged.

This is to weave cobweb, and not cloth. Our friendships hurry to short and poor conclusions, because we have made them a texture of wine and dreams, instead of the tough fibre of the human heart. The laws of friendship are austere and eternal, of one web with the laws of nature and of morals. But we have aimed at a swift and petty benefit, to suck a sudden sweetness. We snatch at the slowest fruit in the whole garden of God, which many summers and many winters must ripen. We seek our friend not sacredly, but with an adulterate passion which would appropriate him to ourselves. In vain. We are armed all over with subtle antagonisms, which, as soon as we meet, begin to play, and translate all poetry into stale prose. Almost all people descend to meet. All association must be a compromise, and, what is worst, the very flower and aroma of the flower of each of the beautiful natures disappears as they approach each other. What a perpetual disappointment is actual society, even of the virtuous and gifted! After interviews have been compassed with long foresight we must be tormented presently by baffled blows, by sudden, unseasonable apathies, by epilepsies of wit and of animal spirits, in the heyday of friendship and thought. Our faculties do not play us true and both parties are relieved by solitude.

I ought to be equal to every relation. It makes no difference how many friends I have and what content I can find in conversing with each, if there be one to whom I am not equal. If I have shrunk unequal from one contest, the joy I find in all the rest becomes mean and cowardly. I should hate myself, if then I made my other friends my asylum:—

> The valiant warrior famousèd for fight,
> After a hundred victories, once foiled,

Is from the book of honor razèd quite
And all the rest forgot for which he toiled.

Our impatience is thus sharply rebuked. Bashfulness and apathy are a tough husk in which a delicate organization is protected from premature ripening. It would be lost if it knew itself before any of the best souls were yet ripe enough to know and own it. Respect the *Naturlangsamkeit* which hardens the ruby in a million years, and works in duration in which Alps and Andes come and go as rainbows. The good spirit of our life has no heaven which is the price of rashness. Love, which is the essence of God, is not for levity, but for the total worth of man. Let us not have this childish luxury in our regards, but the austerest worth; let us approach our friend with an audacious trust in the truth of his heart, in the breadth, impossible to be overturned, of his foundations.

The attractions of this subject are not to be resisted, and I leave, for the time, all account of subordinate social benefit, to speak of that select and sacred relation which is a kind of absolute, and which even leaves the language of love suspicious and common, so much is this purer, and nothing is so much divine.

I do not wish to treat friendships daintily, but with roughest courage. When they are real, they are not glass threads or frostwork, but the solidest thing we know. For now, after so many ages of experience, what do we know of nature or of ourselves? Not one step has man taken toward the solution of the problem of his destiny. In one condemnation of folly stand the whole universe of men. But the sweet sincerity of joy and peace which I draw from this alliance with my brother's soul is the nut itself whereof all nature and all thought is but the husk and shell. Happy is the house that shelters a friend! It might well be built, like a festal bower or arch, to entertain him a single day. Happier, if he know the solemnity of that relation and honor its law! He who offers himself a candidate for that covenant comes up, like an Olympian, to the great games where the first-born of the world are the competitors. He proposes himself for contests where Time, Want, Danger, are in the lists, and he alone is victor who has truth enough in his constitution to preserve the delicacy of his beauty from the wear and tear of all these. The gifts of fortune may be present or absent, but all the speed in that contest depends on intrinsic nobleness and the contempt of trifles. There are two elements that go to the composition of friendship, each so sovereign that I can detect no superiority in either, no reason why either should be first named. One is Truth. A friend is a person with whom I may be sincere. Before him I may think aloud. I am arrived at last in the presence of a man so real and equal that I may drop even those undermost garments of dissimulation, courtesy, and second thought, which men never put off, and may deal with him with the simplicity and wholeness with which one chemical atom meets another. Sincerity is the luxury allowed, like diadems and authority, only to the highest rank; *that* being permitted to speak truth, as having none above it to court or conform unto. Every man alone is sincere. At the entrance of a second person, hypocrisy begins. We parry and fend the approach of our fellow-man by compliments, by gossip, by amusements, by affairs. We cover up our thought from him under a hundred folds. I knew a man who under a certain religious frenzy cast off this drapery, and omitting all compliment and commonplace, spoke to the conscience of every person he encountered, and that with great insight and beauty. At first he was resisted, and all men agreed he was mad.

But persisting—as indeed he could not help doing—for some time in this course, he attained to the advantage of bringing every man of his acquaintance into true relations with him. No man would think of speaking falsely with him, or of putting him off with any chat of markets or reading-rooms. But every man was constrained by so much sincerity to the like plaindealing, and what love of nature, what poetry, what symbol of truth he had, he did certainly show him. But to most of us society shows not its face and eye, but its side and its back. To stand in true relations with men in a false age is worth a fit of insanity, is it not? We can seldom go erect. Almost every man we meet requires some civility—requires to be humored; he has some fame, some talent, some whim of religion or philanthropy in his head that is not to be questioned, and which spoils all conversation with him. But a friend is a sane man who exercises not my ingenuity, but me. My friend gives me entertainment without requiring any stipulation on my part. A friend therefore is a sort of paradox in nature. I who alone am, I who see nothing in nature whose existence I can affirm with equal evidence to my own, behold now the semblance of my being, in all its height, variety and curiosity, reiterated in a foreign form; so that a friend may well be reckoned the masterpiece of nature.

The other element of friendship is Tenderness. We are holden to men by every sort of tie, by blood, by pride, by fear, by hope, by lucre, by lust, by hate, by admiration, by every circumstance and badge and trifle,—but we can scarce believe that so much character can subsist in another as to draw us by love. Can another be so blessed and we so pure that we can offer him tenderness? When a man becomes dear to me I have touched the goal of fortune. I find very little written directly to the heart of this matter in books. And yet I have one text which I cannot choose but remember. My author says,—"I offer myself faintly and bluntly to those whose I effectually am, and tender myself least to him to whom I am the most devoted." I wish that friendship should have feet, as well as eyes and eloquence. It must plant itself on the ground, before it vaults over the moon. I wish it to be a little of a citizen, before it is quite a cherub. We chide the citizen because he makes love a commodity. It is an exchange of gifts, of useful loans; it is good neighborhood; it watches with the sick; it holds the pall at the funeral; and quite loses sight of the delicacies and nobility of the relation. But though we cannot find the god under this disguise of a sutler, yet on the other hand we cannot forgive the poet if he spins his thread too fine and does not substantiate his romance by the municipal virtues of justice, punctuality, fidelity and pity. I hate the prostitution of the name of friendship to signify modish and worldly alliances. I much prefer the company of ploughboys and tin-peddlers to the silken and perfumed amity which celebrates its days of encounter by a frivolous display, by rides in a curricle and dinners at the best taverns. The end of friendship is a commerce the most strict and homely that can be joined; more strict than any of which we have experience. It is for aid and comfort through all the relations and passages of life and death. It is fit for serene days and graceful gifts and country rambles, but also for rough roads and hard fare, shipwreck, poverty and persecution. It keeps company with the sallies of the wit and the trances of religion. We are to dignify to each other the daily needs and offices of man's life, and embellish it by courage, wisdom and unity. It should never fall into something usual and settled, but should be alert and inventive and add rhyme and reason to what was drudgery.

Friendship may be said to require natures so rare and costly, each so well tempered and so happily adapted, and withal so circumstanced (for even in that particular, a poet says, love demands that the parties be altogether paired), that its satisfaction can very seldom be assured. It cannot subsist in its perfection, say some of those who are learned in this warm lore of the heart, betwixt more than two. I am not quite so strict in my terms, perhaps because I have never known so high a fellowship as others. I please my imagination more with a circle of godlike men and women variously related to each other and between whom subsists a lofty intelligence. But I find this law of *one to one* peremptory for conversation, which is the practice and consummation of friendship. Do not mix waters too much. The best mix as ill as good and bad. You shall have very useful and cheering discourse at several times with two several men, but let all three of you come together and you shall not have one new and hearty word. Two may talk and one may hear, but three cannot take part in a conversation of the most sincere and searching sort. In good company there is never such discourse between two, across the table, as takes place when you leave them alone. In good company the individuals merge their egotism into a social soul exactly co-extensive with the several consciousnesses there present. No partialities of friend to friend, no fondnesses of brother to sister, of wife to husband, are there pertinent, but quite otherwise. Only he may then speak who can sail on the common thought of the party, and not poorly limited to his own. Now this convention, which good sense demands, destroys the high freedom of great conversation, which requires an absolute running of two souls into one.

No two men but being left alone with each other enter into simpler relations. Yet it is affinity that determines *which* two shall converse. Unrelated men give little joy to each other, will never suspect the latent powers of each. We talk sometimes of a great talent for conversation, as if it were a permanent property in some individuals. Conversation is an evanescent relation,—no more. A man is reputed to have thought and eloquence; he cannot, for all that, say a word to his cousin or his uncle. They accuse his silence with as much reason as they would blame the insignificance of a dial in the shade. In the sun it will mark the hour. Among those who enjoy his thought he will regain his tongue.

Friendship requires that rare mean betwixt likeness and unlikeness that piques each with the presence of power and of consent in the other party. Let me be alone to the end of the world, rather than that my friend should overstep, by a word or a look, his real sympathy. I am equally balked by antagonism and by compliance. Let him not cease an instant to be himself. The only joy I have in his being mine, is that the *not mine* is *mine*. I hate, where I looked for a manly furtherance or at least a manly resistance, to find a mush of concession. Better be a nettle in the side of your friend than his echo. The condition which high friendship demands is ability to do without it. That high office requires great and sublime parts. There must be very two, before there can be very one. Let it be an alliance of two large, formidable natures, mutually beheld, mutually feared, before yet they recognize the deep identity which, beneath these disparities, unites them.

He only is fit for this society who is magnanimous;

who is sure that greatness and goodness are always economy; who is not swift to intermeddle with his fortunes. Let him not intermeddle with this. Leave to the diamond its ages to grow, nor expect to accelerate the births of the eternal. Friendship demands a religious treatment. We talk of choosing our friends, but friends are self-elected. Reverence is a great part of it. Treat your friend as a spectacle. Of course he has merits that are not yours, and that you cannot honor if you must needs hold him close to your person. Stand aside; give those merits room; let them mount and expand. Are you the friend of your friend's buttons, or of his thought? To a great heart he will be a stranger in a thousand particulars, that he may come near in the holiest ground. Leave it to girls and boys to regard a friend as property, and to suck a short and all-confounding pleasure, instead of the pure nectar of God.

Let us buy our entrance to this guild by a long probation. Why should we desecrate noble and beautiful souls by intruding on them? Why insist on rash personal relations with your friend? Why go to his house, or know his mother and brother and sisters? Why be visited by him at your own? Are these things material to our covenant? Leave this touching and clawing. Let him be to me a spirit. A message, a thought, a sincerity, a glance from him, I want, but not news, nor pottage. I can get politics and chat and neighborly conveniences from cheaper companions. Should not the society of my friend be to me poetic, pure, universal and great as nature itself? Ought I to feel that our tie is profane in comparison with yonder bar of cloud that sleeps on the horizon, or that clump of waving grass that divides the brook? Let us not vilify, but raise it to that standard. That great defying eye, that scornful beauty of his mien and action, do not pique yourself on reducing, but rather fortify and enhance. Worship his superiorities; wish him not less by a thought, but hoard and tell them all. Guard him as thy counterpart. Let him be to thee for ever a sort of beautiful enemy, untamable, devoutly revered, and not a trivial conveniency to be soon outgrown and cast aside. The hues of the opal, the light of the diamond, are not to be seen if the eye is too near. To my friend I write a letter and from him I receive a letter. That seems to you a little. Me it suffices. It is a spiritual gift, worthy of him to give and of me to receive. It profanes nobody. In these warm lines the heart will trust itself, as it will not to the tongue, and pour out the prophecy of a godlier existence than all the annals of heroism have yet made good.

Respect so far the holy laws of this fellowship as not to prejudice its perfect flower by your impatience for its opening. We must be our own before we can be another's. There is at least this satisfaction in crime, according to the Latin proverb;—you can speak to your accomplice on even terms. *Crimen quos inquinat, æquat.* To those whom we admire and love, at first we cannot. Yet the least defect of self-possession vitiates, in my judgment, the entire relation. There can never be deep peace between two spirits, never mutual respect, until in their dialogue each stands for the whole world.

What is so great as friendship, let us carry with what grandeur of spirit we can. Let us be silent,—so we may hear the whisper of the gods. Let us not interfere. Who set you to cast about what you should say to the select soul, or how to say anything to such? No matter how ingenious, no matter how graceful and bland. There are innumerable degrees of folly and wisdom, and for you to say aught is to be frivolous. Wait, and thy heart shall speak. Wait until the necessary and everlasting overpowers you, until day and night avail themselves of your lips. The only reward of virtue is virtue; the only way to have a friend is to be one. You shall not come nearer a man by getting into his house. If unlike, his soul only flees the faster from you, and you shall never catch a true glance of his eye. We see the noble afar off and they repel us; why should we intrude? Late,—very late,—we perceive that no arrangements, no introductions, no consuetudes or habits of society would be of any avail to establish us in such relations with them as we desire,—but solely the uprise of nature in us to the same degree it is in them; then shall we meet as water with water; and if we should not meet them then, we shall not want them, for we are already they. In the last analysis, love is only the reflection of a man's own worthiness from other men. Men have sometimes exchanged names with their friends, as if they would signify that in their friend each loved his own soul.

The higher the style we demand of friendship, of course the less easy to establish it with flesh and blood. We walk alone in the world. Friends such as we desire are dreams and fables. But a sublime hope cheers ever the faithful heart, that elsewhere, in other regions of the universal power, souls are now acting, enduring and daring, which can love us and which we can love. We may congratulate ourselves that the period of nonage, of follies, of blunders and of shame, is passed in solitude, and when we are finished men we shall grasp heroic hands in heroic hands. Only be admonished by what you already see, not to strike leagues of friendship with cheap persons, where no friendship can be. Our impatience betrays us into rash and foolish alliances which no god attends. By persisting in your path, though you forfeit the little you gain the great. You demonstrate yourself, so as to put yourself out of the reach of false relations, and you draw to you the first-born of the world,—those rare pilgrims whereof only one or two wander in nature at once, and before whom the vulgar great show as spectres and shadows merely.

It is foolish to be afraid of making our ties too spiritual, as if so we could lose any genuine love. Whatever correction of our popular views we make from insight, nature will be sure to bear us out in, and though it seem to rob us of some joy, will repay us with a greater. Let us feel if we will the absolute insulation of man. We are sure that we have all in us. We go to Europe, or we pursue persons, or we read books, in the instinctive faith that these will call it out and reveal us to ourselves. Beggars all. The persons are such as we; the Europe, an old faded garment of dead persons; the books, their ghosts. Let us drop this idolatry. Let us give over this mendicancy. Let us even bid our dearest friends farewell, and defy them, saying, "Who are you? Unhand me: I will be dependent no more." Ah! seest thou not, O brother, that thus we part only to meet again on a higher platform, and only be more each other's because we are more our own? A friend is Janus-faced; he looks to the past and the future. He is the child of all my foregoing hours, the prophet of those to come, and the harbinger of a greater friend.

I do then with my friends as I do with my books. I would have them where I can find them, but I seldom use them. We must have society on our own terms and admit or exclude it on the slightest cause. I cannot afford to speak much with my friend. If he is great he makes me so great that I cannot descend to converse. In the great days, presentiments hover before me in the firmament. I ought then to dedicate myself to them. I go in that I may seize them, I go out that I may seize them. I fear only that I may lose them receding into the sky in which now they are only a patch of brighter light. Then, though I prize my friends, I cannot afford to talk with them and study their visions, lest I lose my own. It would indeed give me a certain household joy to quit this lofty seeking, this spiritual astronomy or search of stars, and come down to warm sympathies with you; but then I know well I shall mourn always the vanishing of my mighty gods. It is true, next week I shall have languid moods, when I can well afford to occupy myself with foreign objects; then I shall regret the lost literature of your mind, and wish you were by my side again. But if you come, perhaps you will fill my mind only with new visions; not with yourself but with your lustres, and I shall not be able any more than now to converse with you. So I will owe to my friends this evanescent intercourse. I will receive from them not what they have but what they are. They shall give me that which properly they cannot give, but which emanates from them. But they shall not hold me by any relations less subtle and pure. We will meet as though we met not, and part as though we parted not.

It has seemed to me lately more possible than I knew, to carry a friendship greatly, on one side, without due correspondence on the other. Why should I cumber myself with regrets that the receiver is not capacious? It never troubles the sun that some of his rays fall wide and vain into ungrateful space, and only a small part on the reflecting planet. Let your greatness educate the crude and cold companion. If he is unequal, he will presently pass away; but thou art enlarged by thy own shining, and no longer a mate for frogs and worms, dost soar and burn with the gods of the empyrean. It is thought a disgrace to love unrequited. But the great will see that true love cannot be unrequited. True love transcends the unworthy object and dwells and broods on the eternal, and when the poor interposed mask crumbles, it is not sad, but feels rid of so much earth and feels its independency the surer. Yet these things may hardly be said without a sort of treachery to the relation. The essence of friendship is entireness, a total magnanimity and trust. It must not surmise or provide for infirmity. It treats its object as a god, that it may deify both.

# NOTES

## MANNERS

This essay is from the Second Series, 1844. The subject of manners always interested Emerson; he has written on it repeatedly. In the published Journal there are twenty direct comments on manners, courtesy, society, and the like that are not later used in the essays and lectures; 1824, 1826 (two), 1833, 1835 (three), 1837 (two), 1839, 1840, 1841, 1842, 1849, 1850, 1851, 1852, 1856, 1858, 1860. In the winter of 1836-37 he gave a lecture on "Manners" in Boston; and in the winter of 1841-2 another, the one which formed the basis of this essay. The next winter in New York in a course on New England he gave a lecture on "New England Manners and Customs." Besides this essay there are several which treat either exclusively or at some length of the same subject: "Behaviour" in *Conduct of Life*, "Social Aims" in *Letters and Social Aims*, "Domestic Life" in *Society and Solitude*. Chapters vi and xi in *English Traits* also give many observations on the subject that throw sidelights on the essay under discussion. He alludes to manners in his letters, most pointedly in one to Elizabeth Hoar (1848), printed in Cabot's *A Memoir*, pp. 550-552. Among the poems called *Elements* is one on manners. Quotations from the entry in the Journal, first cited, show that always manners interested Emerson both as a practical social asset and as a symbol of a great spiritual fact: "It certainly is worth one's while, who considers what sway elegant manners bear in society, and how wealth, genius and moral worth do feel their empire; it becomes a clear command of reason to cultivate them. . . . I speak here of no transient success, but of the manners of a sensible man when they become the chief channel in which a man's sense runs; of those which are the plain index of fine sense and fine feelings, which impress all and offend none. . . . This is a species of second philosophy, and may be termed the philosophy of life."

**Introductory poems.** The first four lines are from Ben Jonson's Masque, *Love Freed from Ignorance and Folly,* the rest from his *Pleasure Reconciled to Virtue.*

**Page 2, line 2. Belzoni, Giovanni Battista** (1778-1823), was an Italian explorer of Egyptian antiquities. In 1819 he published in England an account of his discoveries.

**2, l. 5. rock-Tibboos,** or Tibbus ("Men of the Rocks"), a peculiar people that have somewhat puzzled ethnologists as to their race and speech. They dwell in Borku, or Borgu, a region between the Sahara and Sudan.

**2, l. 9. Bornoos,** inhabitants of Bornu, a country of central Sudan, on the south and west of Lake Chad.

**2, l. 30. Sir Philip Sidney** (1554-1586), an Elizabethan writer and courtier. The "novel" referred to is *Arcadia.*

**2, l. 31. Gentleman.** The evolution of the gentleman in the modern sense is connected with the rise of the individual in history. The following books are offered as suggestions in finding material for discussing this: Gilbert Murray's *Euripides and his Age,* Cicero's *Letters* (E. S. Schuckburgh's translation in four volumes or G. E. Jean's *Life and Letters of Cicero*), Strachan-Davidson's *Cicero,* Mackail's *Latin Literature* (discussion of suppression of liberty in literature under the emperors), J. H. Robinson's *Petrarch,* H. D. Traill's *Social England* (6 volumes) especially the chapters on social life, Rousseau's *Social Contract,* and J. H. Robinson's *The Development of Modern Europe.*

**5, l. 7. Lundy's Lane,** near Niagara Falls, where on July 25, 1814, a drawn battle was fought between the Americans and the British.

**5, l. 15. Lord Falkland** (1610-1643), an English writer, active in politics. Emerson was much interested in the account of Falkland given by Clarendon; see Journal IV, 264.

**5, l. 29. Saladin, Sapor,** et cetera. Emerson is given to the insertion of groups of names, often containing some little known, but all belonging to people to whose lives he owed some flash of inspiration. His reverence for the individual lies at the base of this study of biography. Note other examples of this practice in this book.

**Saladin** (1138-1193), a King of Armenia, famous for his conquests in Egypt, Syria, and against the Christians under Richard the Lionhearted of England; see Scott's *Talisman.*

**Sapor,** a Persian monarch, either of the third or the fourth century A. D., who won against the Romans in the east.

**The Cid,** Ruy Diaz de Bevar, a semi-mythical hero of the Spanish wars against the Moors in the eleventh century, became a hero of romances, ballads and chronicles. His name occurs several times in the Journal. See Southey's *Chronicle of the Cid* and Lockhart's *Spanish Ballads.*

**Julius Cæsar** (102-44 B. C.), **Scipio** (185-129 B. C.), **Alexander** (356-323 B. C.), and **Pericles** (490-420 B. C.) are names from Plutarch's *Lives of Greeks and Romans,* a book which, with the *Morals* of the same author, influenced Emerson deeply. See J. and W. Langhorne's translation of the former, and Goodwin's edition of an English translation of the latter.

**Scipio,** the third great bearer of the name, brother-in-law of the Gracchi, was one of Rome's most praised statesmen and warriors in the days of her earliest foreign conquests. He was a patron of philosophers and poets.

**Pericles,** the great Athenian statesman and patron of philosophy, art, and the drama, receives a finely imaginative interpretation in Landor's *Pericles and Aspasia.*

**6, l. 10. Diogenes** (412-323 B. C.), **Socrates** (c. 470-399 B. C.), and **Epaminondes** (418-362 B. C.) were Greeks, who by reason of their lofty character and the circumstances of their lives, are apt illustrations here. Diogenes, the Cynic, and his frugal life are too well known to need comment. Socrates Emerson vividly characterizes in "Plato; or the Philosopher" in "*Representative Men.*" See his *Apologia* in Jowett's translation of Plato's *Dialogues.* Epaminondes was of a noble but impoverished family. Primarily a general, he would yet have ranked high without his brilliant military career for his purity, uprightness, and high culture.

**6, l, 14. My contemporaries.** Edward Emerson finds himself reminded by this passage of Henry Thoreau.

**7, l. 20. Faubourg St. Germain,** the section of Paris where lived the nobility.

**8, l. 1. Cortez** (1485-1547), the Spanish conqueror of Mexico. See Prescott's *Conquest of Mexico.*

**Nelson** (1758-1805), the British naval hero, who met his

death at the battle of Trafalgar. See Mahan's *Life of Nelson* and Southey's *Nelson.*

**Napoleon** (1769-1821). Emerson was singularly attracted to the French conqueror. There are constant references to him in his works. See "Napoleon; or the Man of Action" in *Representative Men.* The victory of Marengo (June 14, 1800) was of especial importance in Napoleon's career, for it came at the beginning of the first consulate when republican opposition was gathering strongly and might, without this victory to turn the scale, have put an end to his power.

**8, l. 4, Funded talent.** A funded debt is one that has been converted into bonds redeemable in a definite period. It is therefore synonymous with surety of payment.

**8, l. 28. One of the estates.** This term, which really means one of the orders that form a state—the nobility, the clergy, and the people—is most commonly associated with France, where the three estates assembled in a body called the states-general to meet emergencies. The last states-general began the French Revolution.

**11, l. 5. Vich Ian Vohr.** See Scott's *Waverley*, chapter 16.

**12, l. 3. Amphitryon,** a hero of Greek mythology, subject of a lost tragedy by Sophocles and of comedies by Plautus and Molière. From a line in the latter's comedy, "Le véritable Amphitryon est l'Amphitryon où l'on dîne," the name has become synonymous with a generous host.

**12, l. 10. Tuileries,** palace and garden of the late French empire, situated in the heart of Paris.

**12, l. 10. Escurial,** a very remarkable Spanish building of the late sixteenth century. It is thirty miles northwest of Madrid.

**13, l. 1. Madame de Staël** (1766-1817), the French novelist and essayist, was the most distinguished and typical product of the period of sensibility.

**13, l. 8. Hazlitt, William** (1778-1830), was an English essayist and critic. He made an English translation of the essays of Montaigne that took the place of the translation that was put out in the late seventeenth century by Cotton. It was the old Cotton translation, however, that fell into Emerson's hands in his early days out of college.

**13, l. 9. Montaigne, Michel de** (1533-1592), invented and perfected the essay as we know it in modern literature. To

Emerson he stands as a mind excellent for its questioning attitude. His critical estimate of Montaigne in *Representative Men* is the most masterly in the English language

**15, l. 32. dry light.** Pure light.

**16, l. 4. Creole natures.** The creoles of Louisiana, descendants of old French settlers, are shown in the delightful pages of G. W. Cable's *Old Creole Days*.

**16, l. 34. Fox, Charles James** (1749-1806), an English statesman and orator, was uniformly opposed in the years 1774-1782 to North's project of coercion of the colonies. Later as a supporter of the French Revolution he was a sturdy opponent of Pitt and became exceedingly unpopular from 1790-1800. The scene alluded to here occurred May 6, 1791.

**18, l. 16. like Circe.** She turned the followers of Odysseus into swine by her magic cup. See Butcher and Lang's translation of Homer's *Odyssey*, Book X. The use of "horned" gives a comical turn to the humor of the passage.

**18, l. 20. Captain Symmes,** a real person. All the others are fictitious names. Symmes claimed to have discovered a flowery path into the earth.

**18, l. 31. the clerisy,** the educated class, or scholars in the wide sense in which Emerson used that word.

**19, l. 18. The epitaph of Sir Jenkins Grant.** The source of this has never been traced. Mr. Edward Emerson thinks it unlikely that his father composed it.

**19, l. 29. Some friend of Poland.** The partition of Poland in 1772 among the three powers, Russia, Prussia, and Austria, and its constantly recurring efforts for freedom, aroused great interest and sympathy among the liberty lovers of Europe, especially after the revolt of 1830 when Europe was filled with Polish exiles.

**19, l. 29. Philhellene,** a lover of the Greeks. The Greek uprising against the Turks in 1821 roused much sympathy and help from other nations. The best known Philhellene was Lord Byron, who died in 1824 at Missolonghi, whither he had gone to take active part with the Greeks.

**20, l. 17. "As Heaven and Earth"** etc., Keats, *Hyperion*, Book II.

**20, l. 27. Ethnical circle,** a group bound together by common characteristics.

**22, l. 33. Minerva,** in Greek Athene, was the goddess of wisdom and womanly skill. **Juno,** in Greek Hera, was among the Romans the protective principle of womanhood in maiden, wife, and mother. **Polymnia,** or Polyhymnia, was the muse of sacred hymns. There is probably significance in Emerson's use of precisely these three names as typical of the ideal woman of action and thought.

**23, l. 4. Delphic Sibyls.** There was a Delphian Sibyl among the ten mentioned by Lactantius. Plato, however, speaks of but one Sibyl. The most famous was the Erythraean at Cumae, whom Æneas consulted in the sixth book of the *Æneid.* It is probable that Emerson means the Pythian priestess who voiced the oracle at Delphi.

**23, l. 15. Hafiz** was the nom de plume of Shams-ud-din Mohammed, a native of Shiraz. He died about 1388. His poetry is lyrical, full of fervent love and splendid nature descriptions, which some interpret mystically; for Hafiz was a dervish. John Richardson brought out *A Specimen of Persian Poetry* in London in 1802, in which were translations of some of Hafiz's poems; but Emerson knew them through the German and the French.

**23, l. 15. Firdousi** was the nom de plume of Abri'l Kasim Mansur, a Persian poet of the tenth century A. D., who wrote a poetic history of Persia, "The Book of the Kings," of which an English abridgment was published in London in 1832. Arnold's *Sohrab and Rustum* is one incident from the poem. Firdousi also wrote a Persian version of the story of Joseph and Potiphar's wife.

**23, l. 29. the seven poets.** Seven was a sacred number among the Persians. The poets referred to here are the seven mystics. The first died about 874 A. D., and the last 1317.

**24, l. 10. the Golden Book,** a traditionary element in fairy lore and tales. *The Golden Book of Venice* preserves the name today.

**25, l. 18. Osman** appears in Emerson's Journal and published writings as an ideal man meant to represent Emerson as he wished to be.

**26, l. 2.** The fable was original with Emerson.

**26, l. 4. Silenus,** a satyr of Roman mythology.

## SELF-RELIANCE

This is an essay from the First Series, 1841. Edward Emerson, tracing the idea of self-reliance in his father's Journal of 1832 makes this comment, "Thus it appears that the writings of Landor, read the year before Mr. Emerson sought him out in Rome, may have given the original push toward the writing of this essay on *Self-Reliance*." The suggestion is interesting. In 1830, a year especially marked for new literary influences in Emerson's life—Goethe, Carlyle, Confucius, Zoroaster—he read some of Landor's *Imaginary Conversations*. The characterizations impressed him. "He has the merit of not explaining" he said, "he writes for the immortals." Entries on self-reliance began in the Journal of 1828; from 1830 they grew more numerous and closer in meaning to the ideas here. Some of this essay appeared in the Journal of 1832; other parts are from the following lectures;—*Individualism* from the Boston course of 1836-37; *School, Genius, Duty,* from the Boston course of 1838-39. In connection with this read the essays on *Character, Heroism, Politics, The American Scholar, The Divinity School Address*.

**27.** The Latin motto is from Persius, *Satire I*, 7. "Seek naught outside thyself." The first poem, from Beaumont and Fletcher, two of Shakespeare's most famous contemporaries, depicts man as the perfect master of his fate. The second, Emerson's own composition, is an allusion to the story of Romulus and Remus. It emphasizes the effect of self-reliance on the individual himself. The exact bearing of each on the lesson of the essay is worthy of study.

**27, l. 1.** Emerson strikes at the start the note of the dignity and importance of the individual and his place in the world. Compare the various ways in which the same idea is looked at in the paragraphs that follow.

**27, l. 1. an eminent painter.** This may mean Washington Allston or Christopher Pearse Cranch. Both wrote verses as well as painted, and both were personally known to Emerson.

**30, l. 23. Lethe,** the underworld river of forgetfulness from which the dead drank that they might remember no more their life on earth.

**30, l. 31.** The contrast between "private" and "necessary" is worthy of note. The "necessary" to Emerson is what in man's thought and action springs from Reason.

**31, l. 20. If I am the Devil's child etc.** This extreme expression of Emerson's independence of thought must be accepted with the mental reservation that he knew he was *not* the Devil's child, and so means only that he will give no one right of judgment over the right and wrong of his actions. "It is when a man does not listen to truth but to others that he is depraved and misled." Journal II, 310.

**36, l. 9. Joseph.** See *Genesis* XXXIX.

**36, l. 22. Pythagoras, Socrates,** etc., all suffered from opposition, more or less violent. Pythagoras (582-500 B. C.) was exiled. Socrates (470-399 B. C.) was condemned to death by a public trial. Luther (1483-1546) was excommunicated. Copernicus (1473-1543) was laughed to scorn and persecuted by the church. Galileo (1564-1642) was imprisoned by the Inquisition. Newton (1642-1727) struggled long for acceptance.

**36, l. 31. acrostic.** See the Dictionary. Does Emerson use the word correctly?

**37. l. 1.** Note the emphasis that must be given "honest" not to misread this paragraph.

**38, l. 1. Chatham.** William Pitt, Earl of Chatham (1708-1778), was a noted English statesman and orator, who upheld the rights of the Americans in opposition to Lord North.

**38, l. 3. Adams's eye.** Samuel Adams, the Revolutionary orator and patriot.

**39, l. 7. Fox, George** (1624-1691), was the founder of Quakerism, first known as the Friends' Society of England. Emerson was much impressed by the Quaker faith. He had a dear friend, Mary Rotch, among them.

**Wesley, John** (1703-1791), was an English evangelist whose preaching stirred all England. He was the founder of Methodism. See Southey's *Life of Wesley*.

**Clarkson, Thomas** (1760-1846), was the man largely instrumental in the passing of an act of Parliament against the slave trade.

**39, l. 8. "the height of Rome,"** Milton, *Paradise Lost*, IX, 510.

**39, l. 24. That popular fable of the sot** is a story used often. There are versions of it in *Arabian Nights* and in Shakespeare's

*Taming of the Shrew,* Induction. Is its use here completely appropriate? Why?

**40, l. 5. Scanderbeg,** or Iskander Bey, was really George Castriota (1403-1468). He was an apostate from the faith of Mahomet, and turned his warlike powers against the Turks.

**Gustavus II** (1594-1632), the great king of Sweden, was a noted soldier and a wise and prudent ruler.

**40, l. 25. Trustee.** Here means the one trusted, as "employee" means the one employed.

**40. l. 27. parallax.** By moving from one place to another a person may create an apparent displacement of a heavenly body. To astronomers this apparent displacement furnishes a basis of measurement for the size and distance of the star or planet. "Without parallax" signifies an extreme distance; here it has the connotation of mystery.

**40, l. 32. Spontaneity, Instinct, Intuition.** These words are synonyms of Reason. See the *Introduction*, p. xxiv.

**41, l. 29. perceptions** Emerson uses to mean the revelations that come to the mind by Intuition, as opposed to knowledge gained by a conscious process of thought.

**43, l. 15. David, Jeremiah, Paul** stand for the authority of the past to which Emerson felt there was a too blind adherence.

**44, l. 9. from man, not to man.** The constant insistence on spiritual solitude for true independence is to be noted.

**44, l. 28. Becomes** here means cessation of motion. To deny the active union of the Great of the past with the Reason of the universe is to refuse the lesson they teach.

**45, l. 16. impure action.** The divine Reason acts on men engaged in helpful, necessary work, often without their will. Pure action would mean action through a mind consciously and perfectly yielding itself to Intuition.

**46, l. 27. Thor,** the thundergod of the Scandinavian mythology, was likewise the god of warlike courage. Woden, his father, was the king of the gods, mighty and prudent.

**47, l. 30. antinomianism** is the opinion that Christians by reason of justification by faith are freed from all necessity to observe the Divine law. For a pleasant picture of an antinomian see George Borrow, *Lavengro,* chapter XXIII.

**50, l. 16. Bonduca,** by John Fletcher is based on the struggle of the Britons against the Roman legions in the first century A. D. The leaders were Caractacus and Boadicea, of two different tribes. They appear as Caratach and Bonduca in the play.

**50, l. 25.** Emerson used no word superfluously; the adverb "foolishly" is emphatic.

**51, l. 4. Zoroaster** founded the old religion of Persia. In 1830 Emerson became acquainted with the teachings of Zoroaster through the works of De Gerando and Auquetil Duperron.

**51, l. 14. Locke, Lavoisier, etc.** John Locke (1632-1704), author of the *Essay on the Human Understanding* and certain treatises on civil and religious liberty. He repudiates innate ideas and intuition as a source of knowledge, and substitutes a gradual acquisition of ideas by experience.

Antoine Lavoisier (1743-94) was the founder of modern chemistry. He proved by experimenting with the balance that chemical change affects the composition without reducing the amount of matter. He proved also that every chemical change may be represented by an equation, and other facts of importance in regard to compounds.

James Hutton (1726-1797) was an eminent geologist. His *Theory of the Earth with Proofs and Illustrations* appeared in 1795.

Jeremy Bentham (1748-1832), the great English utilitarian, set out in a number of remarkable books principles of moral legislation and political economy. His favorite phrase, which serves as a keynote to his teaching is "the greatest happiness for the greatest number."

Johann Spurzheim (1776-1832) was a phrenologist much better known in Emerson's day than in ours. He died in Boston soon after coming there from Germany to deliver leetures.

**51, l. 23. Calvinism,** a sect of Christianity founded by John Calvin (1509-1564) held the belief in predestination.

**Swedenborgism** was the teaching of Emanuel Swedenborg (1698-1772). See Emerson's essay on him in *Representative Men.*

**52, l. 21.** the wise man stays at home etc.

"Nor scour the seas nor sift mankind
A poet or a friend to find.
Behold he watches at the door!
Behold his shadow on the floor!"—*Saadi*, Emerson.

**54, l. 11. Bacon, Francis** (1561-1626), the famous Elizabethan statesman and man of letters. His philosophical work contributed much to arouse the spirit of careful experiment and scientific methods in observation. His essays are among the finest in our language. Compare his essay on *Friendship* with Emerson's on the same subject.

**54, l. 21. chisel of Phidias.** Phidias, born about 500 B.C., was the greatest sculptor of Greece. The names of Phidias, The Egyptian, Moses, and Dante here stand for the highest inspiration in religious art, architecture and literature.

**56, l. 8. Phocion** (c.402-317 B. C.), an Athenian general of humble birth. See Plutarch's *Lives*.

**Anaxagoras** (c.500-428 B. C.) was the last of the old Ionic philosophers, teacher to Pericles, Euripides, and possibly Socrates. He defined a new principle, mind, as working in matter.

**56, l. 15. Hudson, Henry** (d.1611), a navigator who discovered the river and bay that bear his name.

**56, l. 15. Behring, Vitus** (1680-1741), a Danish discoverer for whom Behring Strait and Sea were named.

**56, l. 16. Parry and Franklin** were Arctic explorers early in the last century.

**56, l. 27. Bivouac.** For Emerson's account of Napoleon's methods in war see *Representative Men*. Count de las Cases went with Napoleon to St. Helena and wrote an account of the exile, *Mémoriel de Ste. Hélène.* "Las Casas" is a mistake on Emerson's part.

**57, l. 26. Caliph Ali** (600-661) was a cousin of Mahomet, and his first convert. See Carlyle's *Heroes and Hero Worship.* The maxims and poems attributed to him are pronounced by scholars to be largely of later origin.

**58, l. 20. Cause and Effect, the chancellors of God.** That is the laws are themselves the judges against those who violate them.

## COMPENSATION

This essay appeared in the First Series, 1841. As early as 1823 entries on this subject begin to appear in the Journal. The greatest interest is shown from 1830 on. The essay was probably not prepared as a lecture, though a little of it appeared in the lecture *Duty* of the Boston course of 1838–39. *Prudence* offers some points that bear on the subject.

**59, l. 1.** Note the union of the practical and the ideal in the first three paragraphs. What moral problem is to form the basis of the essay?

**61, l. 20. Polarity.** The word "pole," first used in a scientific sense to signify the extremities of the earth's axis, came during the development of physics to have a much wider meaning, being applied to one of contrasted or opposite parts of a body where a force appears to be concentrated, or to pass in or out of the body. For instance we have the positive and negative poles of a battery. From this meaning of the word was developed the term "polarity," the condition of a body which exhibits opposite powers in opposite directions. Emerson widely extends the meaning to include opposition or contrast in general, sometimes very abstractly. In this and the next five paragraphs Emerson draws in detail the parallel between this law of polarity and the moral law which it symbolizes.

**62, l. 17. Periodic or compensating errors.** The planets are not free from the attractive influence of other planets. This causes periodic deviations in their orbits which are periodically corrected in the natural course of events by recurring changes in the relative positions of the planets.

**64, l. 17.** See Identity and Variety in the *Introduction* for the underlying thought in this and the next paragraph.

**65, l. 30.** Note the idealistic view which makes the "reward or retribution" in the soul that of the "thing or real nature;" and the outer merely circumstantial or apparent.

**65, l. 14.** *It is in the world*, etc. cf. *John* 1.

**65, l. 17.** Oἱ κύβοι Διὸς ἀεὶ εὐπίπτουσι:—Sophocles, Fragments, LXXXIV, 2. "The dice of God fall ever aright."

**67, l. 11. Drive out nature, etc.** A Latin proverb quoted by Horace, Epistles I. 10, 24.

**67, l. 31. "How secret art thou;"**—St. Augustine, Confessions, Book I.

**68, l. 8. Prometheus,** a hero of Greek mythology who brought down the fire of heaven to men and paid the penalty of his boldness by being chained to a rock and preyed upon forever by vultures. He knew a secret fatal to the throne of Zeus, who would free him from his torture if he would impart it. The power and independence of Prometheus has made him a favorite subject with writers of tragedy. Shelley's *Prometheus Unbound* is a modern treatment of the subject. Emerson says of Prometheus: "His story seems to be the first chapter of the history of the Caucasian race."

**68, l. 11. "Of all the gods,"** etc.—Æschylus, *Prometheus.*

**68, l. 19. Aurora,** goddess of the dawn, in love with the Trojan prince Tithonus, brother of Priam, begged for him the boon of immortality from Zeus. Forgetting to ask for immortal youth as well, she was forced to see her lover waste away into decrepit old age. Later legends say he was turned into a grasshopper, or rather a cicada.

**68, l. 20.** Achilles and Thetis. This, of course, refers to the well-known story of the infant Achilles dipped into the River Styx.

**68, l. 23.** Siegfried, hero of the Nibelungenlied, vanquished the Nibelungs and brought off their treasure. He was killed from the rear by Hagen.

**68, l. 34. Nemesis,** Greek personification of the surety of punishment that awaits a deviation from divine laws.

**69, l. 2. The Furies** were Electo, Tisiphone, and Megaera, who stung and scourged those condemned in the judgment hall of the lower world.

**69, l. 6. Ajax** and Hector exchanged arms after a single combat in the Trojan plains. See the Iliad (Lang, Leaf and Myer's translation). Book VII.

**69, l. 11.** Theagenes, an athlete of the isle of Thasos.

**72, l. 9. Polycrates.** The story is from Herodotus III, 39-45 and 120-125. Amasis, king of Egypt, was a friend and ally of Polycrates, tyrant of Samos. Alarmed by his friend's unclouded fortune, he sent him word to shun the envy of the gods and spare to them his chiefest treasure. The tyrant listened and threw into the sea a jewel of great price, his emerald ring. In six days it was drawn from the water in a fish which was served at the tyrant's own table. It was a fatal sign. Amasis hastened to break his league of friendship and ere long the tyranny was broken and the tyrant crucified. See Herodotus, 4 volumes, translated by G. Rawlinson.

**72, l. 28. The highest price he can pay for a thing,** etc., an old proverb. In the translation from Ibn Jenim Emerson wrote:

"Two things thou shalt not long for, if thou love a mind serene;—
A woman to thy wife, though she were a crowned queen;
And the second, borrowed money though the smiling lender say
That he will not demand the debt until the Judgment Day."

**75, l. 15. " Winds blow and waters roll "** etc.:—Wordsworth, Sonnet, *September* 1802.

**79, l. 12. Presence of the soul.** Emerson holds that instinctively we measure by the good or positive standard. This is a subsidiary proof of his belief that the good really *is*, and that the bad is nothing.

**79, l. 32. St. Bernard** (1091-1153), the famous Abbot of Clairvaux and a religious writer of power in the Middle Ages.

## NATURE

This essay belongs to the Second Series, 1844. It was prepared from the Journal rather than from the Waterville lecture of 1841 on the *Method of Nature.* Both were based on the same material. A lost lecture of the Boston course of 1843, *Relation to Nature,* was perhaps the real basis of this essay. The first essay on Nature (1836) and the whole body of Emerson's nature poetry are helpful supplementary reading here. Suggested titles from the latter are, *May Day, Nature, Woodnotes, Monadnoc, My Garden, The Titmouse, The Sea Shore, Song of Nature, The Two Rivers* and *Waldensamkeit.* The first selection in *Mosses from an Old Manse* describes in Hawthorne's words some of the scenes about Concord.

The first essay on *Nature* gives the uses of nature to man as follows: I. Commodity: for food, clothing, heat, transportation, which binds society together, etc. II. Beauty: delight in natural forms, delight in noble and graceful acts, delight in the intellectual contemplation of the beautiful order of the universe. III. Language: Nature as a teacher of words, as a teacher of spiritual facts through natural facts by her symbolism, and as a teacher of the Divine Spirit through symbolism. IV. Discipline: Nature as a discipliner of our understanding through the necessity of subjugating her, or of adapting ourselves to her inevitable course.

**83, The rounded world** etc. The key to an understanding of this little poem by Emerson is his doctrine of Identity. The last two lines are an expression of his belief in the upward or perfecting tendency in nature.

**86, l. 9. Villeggiatura.** Such a village festival was held in Concord in 1840, on June 29. Of it Emerson writes: "Today at the cliff we held our Villeggiatura. I saw nothing better than the passage of the river by that dark clump of trees that line that bank in one spot. As the flowing silver reached that point, it darkened, yet every wave celebrated its passage through the shade by one sparkle. But ever the direction of the sparkles was onward, onward." Journal V. 423.

**87, l. 5. Versailles,** the beautiful French palace and park near Paris.

**87, l. 5. Paphos,** an ancient city on the southwest coast of Cyprus, the center of the cult of Venus Aphrodite, who was fabled to have risen there from the foam of the sea. The ruins point to a city of Mycenean grandeur.

**87, l. 5. Ctesiphon,** a large village on the left bank of the Tigris that after 129 B. C. grew to grand proportions by reason of the Parthians' making it their winter quarters. One gigantic building in ruins remains, "the throne of Khosran."

**87, l. 18. Apollo and Diana,** the twin god and goddess, offspring of Leto and Zeus. Among other powers they had as their province the protection of hunting.

**88, l. 3. Tempe,** the beautiful vale of Thessaly, famed in poetry for its natural charm.

**88, l. 6. Como Lake,** a lovely sheet of water in Lombardy, Northern Italy. At the south a promontory cuts it into two arms.

**88, l. 13. Campagna,** the plain about Rome, once covered with parks and country villas.

**90, l. 16. Proteus,** keeper of Poseidon's sea flocks, the famous old man of the sea who could change his form at will. See the Odyssey, Book IV.

**90, l. 28. Mosaic and Ptolemaic schemes.** The former is the account of the creation in *Genesis*. The latter involves the theory that the earth is the center of the universe and the heavenly bodies revolve about it in circles.

**90, l. 34. Flora,** the Roman goddess of flowers and springtime.

**Fauna,** companion goddess to Faunus, an early Italian god of rural, especially farm, life. He was the god of productiveness.

**Ceres,** or Demeter with the Greeks, the goddess of grain and later of fruits and vegetation in general. She was worshipped too as Mother Earth.

**Pomona,** an ancient Italian goddess of fruits and gardens.

**93, l. 16. Franklin, Benjamin** (1706-1790), is referred to here, of course, for his experiments in electrical science. **John Dalton**

(1766-1844) was a great English chemist. His most important investigations were concerning the atomic theory. **Sir Humphrey Davy** (1778-1829) made many important chemical discoveries. He was the inventor of the Davy lamp for miners. **Joseph Black** (1728-1799), a Scotch chemist, discovered that gases, which he called "fixed air," were freed from certain substances by heating them. He thus demonstrated the existence of a gas distinct from common air.

**96, l. 4. Jacob Behmen,** or Boehme (1575-1624), was born near Gorlitz, and was for thirteen years shoemaker in that city. He was a mystic, not given to ecstasy, but to a confident assertion that he "beheld" mysteries though he could not tell them as they really were. Inward illumination was the source of his great religious power. His *Aurora* appeared in 1610, and later other works of mysticism.

**George Fox.** See Note on *page* 39, *line* 7.

**96, l. 6. James Naylor** (c.1617-1660), a soldier and preacher in the army of the Roundheads. George Fox converted him to Quakerism. He let popularity turn his head, and accepted the names of Christ from his followers. He was pilloried, whipped, branded, and imprisoned. Later, repentant, he was received back into Quakerism. His memoirs were reissued in 1800.

**97. l. 28.** What deductions can be made from the remainder of this paragraph as to Emerson's views of society? Compare with the Essays on *Manners* and *Self-reliance.*

**100, l. 8. Œdipus** was the hero of the famous Theban legend. He solved the riddle of the Sphinx and freed the Thebans from the monster, receiving from Creon the boon that involved himself and his family in a horrible destiny. The bitterness of his lot made his story an attractive theme for Greek tragedy. There are five extant tragedies on the subject.

## FRIENDSHIP

This essay belongs to the First Series, 1841. It contains portions of the following lectures—*Society,* from the Boston course of 1836-37, *The Heart* from the Boston course of 1838-39, and *Private Life* from the course of 1839-40. In connection with this essay suggestive reading is found in *Social Aims, Love, Discipline, Heroism.*

**103. A ruddy drop,** etc. In this poem of Emerson is struck a note of dependence on others which is often lacking in his writings. Reconcile the views here expressed with the emphasis he lays later in the essay on the aloofness of the individual.

**105, l. 2.** Emerson's high ideal of the individual brought him often disappointment in his relations with men. "I never get used to men: they always awaken expectations in me which they always disappoint."—Journal III, 100. "Bacon, Shakespeare, Caesar—none of them will bear examination or furnish the type of a man."—Journal II. 505. The idea recurs often. See *English Traits* and *Representative Men.*

**106, l. 21. "crush the sweet poison of misused wine";**—Milton, *Comus.*

**107, l. 16. Elysian temple** would be a temple of the blest in the Elysian fields, the abode of deathless heroes.

**107, l. 24. Egyptian skull.** From Plutarch comes the story that the Egyptians enlivened their feasts by passing a mummy at the close to remind the guests that all must die.

**108, l. 1.** a poor **Greek,** that is a man of taste and sensibility, to be measured by his soul, rather than his outer trappings.

**108, l. 3.** that vast **shadow of the Phenomenal.** A friend, incomparably beyond all else in the world, is yet mysteriously felt a something outside one's being, a symbol only of what the soul itself is. The elusiveness of friendship in this profound sense has been variously treated by poets. See Browning, *Love in a Life.*

**109, l. 33. "The valiant warrior"** etc.:—Shakespeare, Sonnet XXV.

**111, l. 4.** an **Olympian** refers to one trained by the rigorous course that the rules prescribed and presenting himself as a competitor in the famous Olympian games in Elis, Greece.

**111, l. 30. I know a man etc.** Edward Emerson is an authority for the statement that this is a reference to Jones Very. Emerson offers most interesting and sympathetic comments on this curious Transcendental poet. The Centenary Edition quotes two passages, and in the Journal appear several others. One of the most interesting of the latter reads in part as follows:—"Entertain every thought, every character that goes by with the hospitality of your soul. . . . Especially if one of these monotones, whereof, as my friends think, I have a savage society, like a menagerie of monsters, come to you, receive him. For the partial action of his mind in one direction is a telescope for the objects on which it is pointed."—Journal V. 98.

**113, l. 3.** **"I offer myself"** etc.:—Montaigne I. XXXIX. (See his *Essay on Friendship* in comparison with Emerson's.)

**116, l. 27.** **pottage.** See *Genesis* XXV.

**119, l. 24.** **Janus-faced.** Janus, the old Latin god, had two faces.

CPSIA information can be obtained
at www.ICGtesting.com
Printed in the USA
BVHW050525190522
637378BV00001B/54

9 781010 411857